SECRET SEATTLE

A Guide to the Weird, Wonderful, and Obscure

Mary Jo Manzanares

Reedy Press
PO Box 5131
St. Louis, MO 63139
www.reedypress.com

Library of Congress Control Number: 2020950056
ISBN: 9781681063089

All photos by the author unless otherwise noted.

Design by Jill Halpin

We (the publisher and the author) have done our best to provide the most accurate information available when this book was completed. However, we make no warranty, guarantee, or promise about the accuracy, completeness, or currency of the information provided, and we expressly disclaim all warranties, express or implied. Please note that attractions, company names, addresses, websites, and phone numbers are subject to change or closure, and this is outside of our control. We are not responsible for any loss, damage, injury, or inconvenience that may occur due to the use of this book. When exploring new destinations, please do your homework before you go. You are responsible for your own safety and health when using this book.

Printed in the United States of America
21 22 23 24 25   5 4 3 2 1

To Tony and Kaiden, whose love and support are reflected on every page of this book. You are the two people that I most want to explore the world with.

CONTENTS

ACKNOWLEDGMENTS

Writing a book in the middle of a pandemic is a crazy idea. With closure and lockdown policies changing seemingly daily, these secrets were rewritten more times than I can count. At the time of publication, this information was current and accurate. Next week that could all change, so I recommend checking before heading out to explore.

I owe my gratitude to all the public relations representatives, local journalists, historians, librarians, and local experts who answered multiple emails and phone calls, updating me regularly, all while working from home. I can't wait until we can meet up in person again.

To the servers and front desk clerks, the receptionists and janitors, and the office staff who shared their stories, your time and kindness are appreciated.

To the city of Seattle, I love you even though you frustrate me. Like me, you're not perfect, but we muddle through together. Many thanks to Josh at Reedy Press for giving me the opportunity to write this book and to Barbara for helping me through the frequently changing tourism landscape. We finally got there.

And finally, my love and appreciation to my husband, Tony. From serving as my driver to helping with photography and providing feedback, I couldn't have done it without you. And I wouldn't have wanted to, either.

INTRODUCTION

Pssst! I'll let you in on a little secret. In fact, this book is full of secrets.

Secrets are funny things. Over the years, stories change and grow with each re-telling until the origin story becomes lost and forgotten. That's where *Secret Seattle* comes in. I've tracked back details, people, and stories to separate fact from fiction and get the scoop on wonderful destinations, obscure history, and wacky legends in the greater Seattle area. Seattle has a colorful past, full of brothels, ghosts, and shady characters with questionable scruples. It also has a rich cultural past, full of Native American and Asian history, and a diversity that comes from its coastal location.

As a native Washingtonian, I was surprised by how much I didn't know about my city. Niche libraries and museums, historical sites and architecture, local residents, and other oddities were all fair game for exploration. There were lots of opportunities to say, "I didn't know that."

Whether you're a local wanting to learn more about the area or a visitor wanting an offbeat recommendation, *Secret Seattle* starts you off on a path of discovery.

THE PEOPLE'S REPUBLIC OF FREMONT

Why is Fremont the center of the universe?

In 1991, a group of Fremont scientists determined that their neighborhood, specifically the intersection of North Fremont Avenue and 35th Street North, was the universe's geographical center. Somewhat unsurprisingly, this high-level discussion took place in a local bar. While the assertion couldn't be proven, neither could it be disproven. The rationale was simple: "Because we said it is."

Fremont cemented its claim to the title by asking the Metropolitan King County Council for a proclamation declaring it to be so. In 1994, the council declared the Artistic Republic of Fremont to be an Independent ImagiNation and a mecca for people of independent mind and spirit and confirmed that it was, indeed, the Center of the Universe.

A "Center of the Universe" sign was erected to commemorate this important designation. Located on a traffic island at the intersection of North Fremont Avenue and 35th Street North, the directional sign points to landmarks in Fremont and destinations around the world. Louvre? 9,757 km. Milky Way? 69 light-years. Noogie? The top of your head.

While originally a center for counterculture movements, today Fremont has embraced gentrification right along with its

---

The "Center of the Universe" signpost has been knocked down and stolen, but has always been fixed up and replaced by Fremont businesses.

The Fremont "Center of the Universe" sign points the way to destinations around the world (and beyond).

BECAUSE WE SAID SO

WHAT: A Seattle neighborhood

WHERE: North of downtown, along the Fremont Cut of the Lake Washington Ship Canal

COST: Free, except for personal expenditures

PRO TIP: The annual Fremont Walking Guide is distributed at Hysterical Markers throughout the neighborhood.

Bohemian roots. In addition to being the Center of the Universe, Fremont is well known for its Solstice Parade. The parade celebrates the longest day of the year and serves as a celebration of the community's creative expression. The controversial Solstice cyclists unofficially start the parade. Despite the Cyclists wearing more body paint than clothing, the parade remains a family-friendly event.

A FISHY STORY

Where can you see a man kissing a big fish?

There once was a beautiful young maiden who fell in love with a handsome fisherman. As so often happens in stories involving beautiful young maidens, a wicked witch came along and messed things up. In the Legend of the Big Catch, the wicked witch also fell in love with the handsome fisherman and cast a spell that turned the maiden into a fish. The devastated fisherman sailed the Puget Sound waters looking for his one true love. He eventually found her, saved her with a kiss that turned her back into a maiden, and everyone lived happily ever after.

That legend is the story behind the statue *Big Catch*. Or maybe it's not. In the case of the *Big Catch*, it's definitely not. The fish came first, then the legend. Here's how that happened.

Des Moines is located about five miles south of Sea-Tac Airport. As Seattle's population growth spread out from the city center, Des Moines saw population growth. Toward the end of the 20th century, this resulted in traffic headaches. The Department of Transportation was tasked with making improvements, and one of those improvements was to change the traffic flow by creating a new intersection on the west side of Highway 590/Marine View Drive near South 219th Street.

BIG CATCH PLAZA

WHAT: Public art

WHERE: 21634 Marine View Dr. S., Des Moines

COST: Free

PRO TIP: The Washington State city of Des Moines is pronounced with the "s" on the end—duh-moinz.

From a distance, the *Big Catch* statue looks like a man dancing with a fish.

Seattle artist Richard Beyer created the Big Catch *sculpture in Des Moines.*

The construction project created a plaza on the corner. Since every plaza needs art, the city commissioned Seattle artist Richard Beyer to create something that reflected the maritime history of Des Moines. He created a bronze statue of a scruffy fisherman grabbing the human breasts of a very large fish. When controversy ensued, Beyer made up the legend to appease the neighbors and create a romantic story to accompany the statue.

Today the controversy that surrounded the *Big Catch* has mostly been forgotten. Although an occasional motorist will slow down to give it a second look, the statue didn't live up to its notoriety. The legend, however, continues to be told.

BE A PATCHES PAL

Who was the Mayor of the City Dump?

For more than 53 years, Julius Pierpont Patches reigned as mayor of the City Dump. Known simply as J. P., a clown who lived in a shack at the dump, he sported a bright red nose, a colorful patchwork coat, and a tattered hat. As the self-appointed mayor, J. P. hosted the *J. P. Patches Show* and for over 50 years implored kids to mind their parents and be of good moral character.

Two generations of kids grew up on J. P.'s high-energy slapstick humor. He had a girlfriend named Gertrude, frequently fell off his adult-sized tricycle, and looked into viewer homes by using his cardboard ICU2-TV (I See You Too). The zany cast of supporting characters, whether male, female, or animal, were all played by local actor Bob Newman.

J. P. never talked down to kids. That was part of his appeal. While his message was always wholesome, parents got a chuckle over the frequent use of double entendres and witticisms that flew over the heads of their kids.

The show was unscripted and broadcast live on local CBS affiliate KIRO from 1958 to 1981. Scout troops and school groups appeared on the show, introducing themselves to the television audience. While most kids were excited to appear on television, for others it was a sad realization that the shack at the City Dump was just a set at the television station. While J. P. preceded the days of influencers, he influenced generations of kids to wash behind their ears, brush their teeth, and be a clean plate club

CLOWNING AROUND

WHAT: Beloved television character

WHERE: On video, merchandise, and in memories.

COST: It doesn't cost a cent to be a Patches Pal.

PRO TIP: A statue dedicated to J. P. and Gertrude, *Late for the Interurban*, is located in Fremont on North 34th Street.

J. P. and Gertrude rushing to catch the Interurban.

member. His viewers—avid followers—were called Patches Pals, and everyone wanted to be a Patches Pal.

Chris Wedes, who played J. P., continued the role for another 30 years after the show went off the air. Until his death, J. P. made appearances at area festivals, performed at local events, and regularly visited kids in local hospitals.

Because the *J. P. Patches Show* was broadcast live, there is very little footage from the show in real time.

SPREADING THE NEWS

How did founding Asian immigrants keep up on the news?

You probably start your day off with coffee and the news, and then head off for work. You read the newspaper while having your coffee, listen to the radio in the car, or pull up the internet on your mobile device. Regardless of your preferred format, it's easy to get a daily dose of news and community events.

During the late 1800s, immigrants from Asia generally, and from China more specifically, were responsible for much of Seattle's development. Chinese immigrants came to Seattle to work as domestics and service workers supporting the Gold Rush and to build the rail lines. They endured grueling hours and poor working conditions. Language barriers isolated them. Their only source of news and current events was word of mouth.

To mitigate this isolation, the Chinese immigrants created a community bulletin board that performed the function of a newspaper. The bulletin board was rudimentary—an old piece of wood—and was hung on the side of the Louisa Hotel, where many Asian immigrants lived. The area became the center of what was then known as Chinatown, now known as the International District. Immigrants covered the bulletin board with business listings, protest posters, and routine updates from around Seattle posted in Asian languages. It soon became the go-to source for reliable and accurate information for the immigrant community.

Although it was decades before a Chinese-language newspaper was established, the bulletin board fell into disuse and disrepair.

A simple bulletin board connected Seattle's Chinese community long before a Chinese-language newspaper existed.

The Chinese Community Bulletin Board is located on the side of the Louisa Hotel in Seattle's International District.

In the 1960s, the community restored the bulletin board, and in 1976 the City Council declared it a historic landmark. Officially known as the Chinese Community Bulletin Board, it's located at the original site. A tiled overhang protects readers from the Seattle rain.

The bulletin board is no longer covered with news stories. Instead you'll find community announcements and posters for local events. More importantly, though, the bulletin board honors the history and importance of the Chinese community in Seattle.

FINDING COMMUNITY

WHAT: Historic site

WHERE: 511 Seventh Ave.

COST: Free

PRO TIP: During Prohibition, two speakeasies were located in the basement of the Louisa Hotel. Original Art Deco murals are on display at the hotel, now an income-qualified apartment complex.

NOW HEAR THIS

Why was there a weekly siren?

If you were around between the 1950s and the early 1970s, you might have vague memories of sirens going off like clockwork every Wednesday at noon. The Cold War and the fear surrounding the threat of a nuclear attack resulted in air raid towers being installed all over America. In 1952, 21 air raid towers were installed around Seattle; today only two remain.

The Phinney neighborhood tower had a monster siren on top. When it went off, it was loud enough to be heard in a three-mile radius. It was called Big Bertha. The weekly siren was part of a test of the emergency systems. Booklets explained the protocol in case of an attack. Students learned duck-and-cover drills at the nearby school, ducking beneath their desks and covering their heads as protection in case of a surprise attack. The sirens served primarily as security theater. It's widely agreed that in the event of an actual nuclear attack, the siren couldn't have been activated in time.

By the start of the 1970s, the fear surrounding communism and a nuclear attack began to subside. The country no longer needed air raid sirens. The noon sirens stopped, as did the duck-and-cover drills. Big Bertha stood tall and quiet.

The Phinney Air Raid Tower is a relic of the atomic age, a time when the entire country lived in fear of something that never came. It's a symbol of peace, not of war.

The Phinney Air Raid Tower is a relic of the atomic era.

PHINNEY AIR RAID TOWER

WHAT: Historic landmark

WHERE: 6532 Phinney Ave. N.

COST: Free

PRO TIP: The other surviving Seattle air raid tower is located in Northacres Park, although it has not been restored.

A couple of decades later, the neighborhood association decided to restore the Phinney Air Raid Tower to memorialize World War II. The siren got a fresh coat of bright yellow paint, and the tower was painted green. It stands proudly, although still quietly, overlooking the Phinney neighborhood. It's a city landmark and was listed on the Washington Heritage Register of Historic Places in 2011.

A HAUNTED BROTHEL

Where can you have a drink in a former brothel?

Merchants Cafe in Pioneer Square is one of the few surviving establishments from the American expansion period of the 19th century. When a restaurant is as old as a city's folk tales, it will be the subject of many complex and questionable stories.

In 1889, the Great Seattle Fire destroyed Seattle's entire central business district, including the original wooden building. It was rebuilt, along with the rest of the neighborhood, using terra cotta bricks that have become Pioneer Square's hallmark. The building was sold and became the Merchants Exchange Saloon.

Like all good western saloons of the era, it offered rooms for rent by the hour and entertainment beyond the ordinary drinks and bar service. The proprietor, intent on profiting off the lumberjacks' lonely plight and the gold miners passing through Seattle, imported prostitutes to the city. He housed them in the upper rooms of the hotel under the guise of hiring seamstresses. The women's portraits hung at the back of the saloon, and gentlemen could select their partner from them. The portraits are still hanging in the cafe today. It's rumored that the ghost of one woman haunts the women's bathroom.

After its stint as a brothel, the saloon was sold, and the next owner set up a bank—miners returning from the gold rush needed

MERCHANTS CAFE

WHAT: Seattle's oldest standing restaurant and bar

WHERE: 109 Yesler Way

COST: Sandwiches and entrees start at $10.

PRO TIP: Merchants Cafe's carved bar was shipped around Cape Horn in the late 1800s.

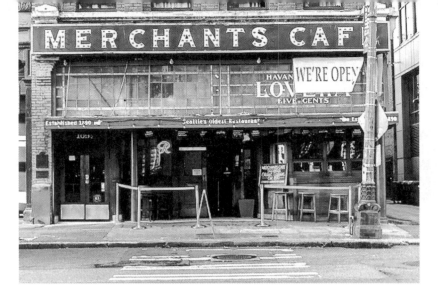

Merchants Cafe is Seattle's oldest standing restaurant and bar.

to exchange their gold dust for cash. It was not unusual for the bank to convert nearly $100,000 worth of gold dust on a busy weekend.

When Prohibition came along, the saloon relocated to the basement, becoming a speakeasy. A gambling hall was added, and it's believed that police were paid to look the other way. Nothing puts a damper on Seattle fun.

Today Merchants Cafe has embraced its racy history while conforming to modern laws. The brothel rooms are now private apartments. The gambling hall is gone, but the 1800s decor and wooden flooring remain. It's no longer a speakeasy, but the carved bar is still in use. And the menu is full of creatively named entrees like Klondike Mac 'n' Cheese and Madam Lou's Meatloaf Dinner.

The Merchants Cafe was designed by W. E. Boone, a direct descendent of Daniel Boone.

STEALING IS WRONG

Where can you find a stolen totem pole?

We teach youngsters that stealing is wrong and that justice always prevails. As we grow up, however, we learn that life is messy and complicated. Complicated is undoubtedly the case with the Chief-of-all-Women totem pole in Pioneer Square.

In 1899, the *Seattle Post-Intelligencer* sponsored an expedition of leading citizens to the District of Alaska. The Seattle Chamber of Commerce sent a committee of prominent businessmen on this goodwill tour to investigate the prospect of increased trade and investment in Alaska.

The expedition set sail with 165 members and included stops in Vancouver, Mary Island, and Glacier Bay. There was also a stop at the Tlingit village at Fort Tongass. The Chamber of Commerce committee members observed many totem poles in the village. Since it appeared deserted, the men decided to take the best totem pole they could find as a souvenir. They chopped down the massive pole, sawed it in half, and took it back to Seattle.

Once back home, the committee gave the totem pole to the city as a gift, claiming it had been abandoned. It was installed in Pioneer Square. But the totem pole hadn't been abandoned, and the village wasn't deserted. Tribal members had merely been away fishing and were upset to find it missing upon their return. An elder of the tribe had witnessed the theft, and a tribal delegation headed off to Seattle to retrieve the totem pole.

Things didn't go so well in Seattle, and the Tlingits could not recover their totem pole. So they filed a federal lawsuit to

The stolen totem pole was publicized as a Seattle tourist attraction during the Alaska-Yukon-Pacific Exposition.

The Chief-of-All-Women totem pole stands among the trees in Pioneer Square.

CHIEF-OF-ALL-WOMEN

WHAT: Public landmark

WHERE: Pioneer Square at 1st Avenue and Yesler Way

COST: Free

PRO TIP: Chief-of-all-Women is one of the few totem poles dedicated to a woman and tells the life story of a Tlingit woman who drowned in the Nass River.

recover damages. That didn't go so well either, and a federal judge dismissed the suit. Eight men were eventually indicted on federal charges of theft and fined only a meager $500, and the city was allowed to keep the totem pole. Such was Seattle justice.

An arsonist torched the totem pole in 1938, and the resulting damage was too extensive for repair. The city commissioned a replica of the original totem, this one paid for, and Tlingit carvers once again did the work. The replica was blessed by the tribe and then sent back to Seattle to stand in Pioneer Square.

PARTY WITH AN ELEPHANT

Where can you rent an elephant?

Taking a world tour, buying tickets to the Olympics, or self-publishing your novel are some of the things you could do with $10,000. In 2009, Larry Steele, the owner of Aurora Rents, decided to invest his ten grand in renovating the life-size concrete elephant on top of his store.

The elephant was built sometime between 1929 and 1936 by tile artisan Giovanni "John" Braida. He wanted to keep his employees busy during the Great Depression and settled on creating a statue to show off their artistry. Braida made the elephant with materials collected from his backyard—chicken wire, reinforced water pipes, and wood. Drawing inspiration from India, he added an ornate carriage called a howdah on top of the elephant's back.

For almost a decade, the elephant stayed with Braida. It stood proudly in front of his shop, where the neighborhood children came to climb and play on it. In 1946, the elephant was installed atop the Aurora Flower Shop. Why an elephant at a flower shop? The marquee sign read, "Elephants have a great memory—do you? Don't forget your wife's birthday!"

When Steele acquired the property and converted it into Aurora Rents, the elephant was in bad shape. By this time, however, the kitschy roadside fixture had become a part of the neighborhood and nobody, including Steele, wanted to see her go. So he hired a concrete contractor to restore Aurora the Elephant to her original state.

Aurora the Elephant was first an art project,
then a marketing and promotional tool,
and finally a neighborhood attraction that
fascinates visitors from around the world.

Although Aurora stands on private property, Aurora Rents welcomes visitors who want to see her.

Aurora was actually in quite a precarious condition. Her concrete was on the verge of falling off, and her wooden elements had begun to rot. Pigeons had made a home in her underbelly. It took months of meticulous cleaning and renovating to complete the repairs. In November 2009, Aurora returned to her spot on top of the rental store sign.

Aurora is listed as a rental item at the store for $10,005, plus all removal, installation, and delivery costs. Plus, the customer must provide some type of zoo animal statue to take her place while she's gone; rhinos and giraffes preferred. You can't rent her. They just have a sense of humor.

ELEVATOR OF THE SPACE AGE

What happened to the World's Fair Bubbleator?

Seattle's 1962 World's Fair was called Century 21. The motto was "Living in the Space Age," and exhibits provided a peek into the future and our buildings, cars, and technology. Some predictions were spot on—cordless phones and teleconferencing—while others missed the mark. We're still waiting for those flying cars.

However, few in the '60s were predicting the surge of environmental trends, nor that green buzzwords would become part of our daily lexicon. There wasn't much talk about "reduce, reuse, recycle" at the fair, but it turns out that the concept saved the beloved Bubbleator.

The Bubbleator was a spherical Plexiglass elevator, about 19 feet in diameter, built for the sole purpose of transporting the guests of Seattle's World's Fair between the floors of the Washington State Coliseum. The name came from combining "bubble" (since it looked like one) and "elevator." One hundred people at a time could fit into the Bubbleator, most riders wanting to jostle to the edges to get a view as it went up and down to the World of Tomorrow exhibit.

Once the fair ended, the Bubbleator moved to the Center House, where the old Food Circus was located, and remained popular. On Halloween the sphere was turned into a pumpkin, and during Christmas it became a snowman. After nearly two decades of

---

BUBBLEATOR

WHAT: Artifact from the 1962 World's Fair

WHERE: 28708 Sound View Dr. S., Des Moines

COST: Free

PRO TIP: *The Bubbleator Sessions*, an album recorded by local band Trip Like Animals, was recorded inside the Bubbleator to celebrate the 50th anniversary of the World's Fair.

The Bubbleator from the Seattle World's Fair is now a greenhouse.

service, the Bubbleator was retired and donated to Children's Hospital. The hospital couldn't find a use for it, and it languished in pieces in a storeroom.

Local newspaperman Gene Achziger discovered the fate of the Bubbleator while researching a story for the 50th anniversary of the World's Fair. When he found that it was lying unused in a warehouse, he decided to buy it and move it to his home. It was a bargain at $1,000, but it took tens of thousands of dollars more to transport and reassemble it in his front yard.

The Bubbleator has been recycled into a greenhouse. It's easy to spot when you're driving in the neighborhood, but it's a private residence, so visitors have to gawk from the street.

In the six months that the Seattle World's Fair was open, over two and a half million people rode the Bubbleator.

THE PLAY THAT ROCKED SEATTLE

Did the Seahawks cause an earthquake?

The NFL's Seattle Seahawks are known for the support of their fans. Twice, fans have set the Guinness World Record for the loudest crowd noise at a sporting event. But can Seattle fans make the earth move?

Yes!

The first occurrence, setting the benchmark for all fan activity to follow, was during a home game against the New Orleans Saints on January 8, 2011. A 67-yard touchdown run by running back Marshawn Lynch brought fans to their feet, jumping and shouting at the imminent victory. Fans were amazed. Equally remarkable, the enthusiastic supporters created ground vibrations that were substantial enough to set off equipment at a nearby seismic station. The M=2 tremor registered at Qwest Field (now known as Lumen Field).

The human-made earthquake became known as Beast Quake, named for Lynch, whose running style was called "beast mode."

Following Beast Quake, the Pacific Northwest Seismic Network set up seismometers around the stadium to register "fan quakes" in real time. Additional fan quakes have been recorded, including after an October 29, 2017, game-winning touchdown pass from Russell Wilson to tight end Jimmy Graham in a game against the Houston Texans.

After its implosion in 2000, 100 percent of the concrete from the Kingdome was processed and recycled. Approximately 50 percent of that was used to build Lumen Field.

Lumen Field is an open-air stadium and is home to the Seattle Seahawks and the Seattle Sounders.

BEAST QUAKE

WHAT: Seismic activity at a Seahawks game

WHERE: Lumen Field, 800 Occidental Ave. S.

COST: Free to watch from home. Tours of Lumen Field are $14.

PRO TIP: You can watch game day seismic activity live at quickshake.pnsn.org.

While human-made earthquakes mean Seahawk fans can make the earth move, Seattle doesn't need to worry that these are going to set off the "big one." Significantly, though, these fan quake readings—and the way the measurements get relayed in real time—are of value to scientists planning for the big one.

THE LAST HOLDOUT

Why is there an abandoned house in the middle of a shopping center?

For a million dollars, many of us would gladly part with a prized possession. However, the same could not be said for Edith Macefield when it came to her century-old Ballard home. In 2006, when Macefield's neighborhood experienced rapid growth, she was approached by developers looking to buy her property for their five-story commercial project. She declined the offer numerous times, even though the offer grew to a million dollars.

The other neighbors sold their lots, and the developer eventually built Ballard Blocks around the Macefield house. It became surrounded on three sides by the shopping center's concrete walls, leaving only the front yard open.

The press loved the odd sight, and the story appeared on the front page of the *New York Times*. Her small home, surrounded by extensive commercial development, made Macefield a celebrity and a symbol of resistance against development. It prompted conversations about the effects of urban development on history and culture and about the evolution of communities, and it created an underdog story worth cheering.

As for Macefield herself, she wanted no part in all the media attention. All she wanted to do was spend her remaining life in the only home she had known. She struck up a friendship with

---

The Disney movie *Up* was not based on the Macefield House, although they did use it to publicize the 2009 movie. A Macefield House movie is reportedly under development, though.

The Macefield House in Ballard is currently abandoned.

THE MACEFIELD HOUSE

WHAT: An abandoned home

WHERE: 1438 NW 46th St.

COST: Free

PRO TIP: Curtis James, a local artist at Anchor Tattoo, designed a Macefield House tattoo with the world "Steadfast" at the bottom.

Barry Martin, the Ballard Blocks project superintendent, and it was not unusual for the two to have lunch together during the construction. For the final two years of her life, Martin became Macefield's primary caregiver, and as her last act, Macefield bequeathed the home to him.

Over the years that followed, the property changed hands several times, and with each change the uncertainty regarding the fate of the little house loomed. Its future is still unknown. For now, the house remains locked and fenced off while it continues to fall into disrepair.

When Macefield refused to give up her home, she didn't know that her house would come to symbolize the gentrification battle that had racked the city for nearly two decades. All she wanted to do was live out the remainder of her days on her terms, in her own house. However, through her resistance, she became an anti-establishment hero in Seattle, and her determination is still celebrated.

SINGING PRAISES

What is the chanting coming from St. Mark's?

At 9:30 p.m. on any Sunday night, you'll find casually dressed people sitting in the dark at St. Mark's Episcopal Cathedral. They may be scattered among the pews or lying on the concrete floor, but chances are they'll be deep in contemplation as they soak up the music of the Compline Choir. It's a chance to look inward and reflect on where you are in life, doing so in a respectful and non-denominational environment.

The choir's roots began in 1956 when Peter Hallock invited 12 music students from the University of Washington to study and sing sacred music, including plainsong, the unharmonized liturgical chant of medieval Europe. Under Hallock's musical direction, the group went on to form an official choir and began singing the compline, the last service of the day. The compline follows a specific order of hymns, psalms, scriptures, and prayer.

Initially the nave was empty, with few people attending services. However, the counterculture movement of the 1960s, and the accompanying interest in alternative spiritual practices like meditation and Eastern chanting, began drawing young, esoteric crowds to hear the choir. For decades, compline guests were predominantly young, giving the church the reputation of being unconventional.

Believing that one way to God was through song, Hallock emphasized mindfulness over any specific doctrine. He composed

---

COMPLINE CHOIR

WHAT: Musical worship services

WHERE: St. Mark's Episcopal Cathedral, 1245 10th Ave. E.

COST: Free, donations appreciated

PRO TIP: Compline services are broadcast live on KING-FM 98.1, and the Compline Choir podcast is available on most podcasting platforms.

The Compline Choirs sing at St. Mark's Episcopal Cathedral.

over 250 liturgical works, including some widely used in Episcopal and Lutheran services. Under his nearly 50 years of leadership, the Compline Choir and services have not only achieved national prominence but also revived public interest in the ritualistic singing of praise.

Since 2003, the Compline Choir has been under Jason Anderson's direction. He continues to develop public interest in the choir and services. The choir travels internationally to great acclaim, and since 2019 the women's compline choir has become more integrated into services.

Women broke a glass ceiling in 2019 when the Women's Compline Choir sang the service for the first time.

AS FAST AS A GREASED LOG ROLLING DOWNHILL

Where was the first skid row?

The Denny Party arrived in the hilly lands of early timber town Seattle in 1851. No sooner had they made their way to the waterfront than they invited Henry Yesler, a wealthy entrepreneur from Ohio, to set up his new steam-powered sawmill in the town.

After buying land from pioneer Doc Maynard, Yesler set up his mill on Elliott Bay. Timber was sent to the mill by greasing the logs, then skidding them down a long, steeply sloped road, in this case.

SEATTLE'S SKID ROW

WHAT: An intersection that divided a neighborhood

WHERE: Western Avenue and Yesler Way

COST: Free

PRO TIP: The term was originally Skid Road; later it was shortened to Skid Row.

And that is how Yesler Way became this country's first skid road. With time, this road became the separator between Seattle's affluent society and the impoverished populations, including the mill workers and other members of the working class. Today we know it as Pioneer Square.

Pioneer Square prospered under the influence of diverse cultures and ethnicities until the Great Seattle Fire of 1889 burned everything to the ground. The fire damaged nearly 100 acres of the business district, and losses soared. Seattle-ites vowed to rebuild, marking a turning point in the history of the city.

Under strict fireproof building codes, Pioneer Square was rebuilt in brick, stone, and iron, with a visible unity of appearance. The streets were raised, grades were leveled; the neighborhood was built to last. Many of the post-fire buildings stand to this day.

In 1897, Seattle became an essential point of travel to and from the gold-rich Yukon Valley. Although very few made their fortune from the gold rush, it led to a boom in Seattle's economy. Pioneer

The intersection at Western Avenue and Yesler Way in Pioneer Square

Square merchants made profits by supplying and sheltering the often gruff and burly miners, furthering the Skid Row class divide.

As Seattle's Central Business District expanded north, Pioneer Square's economy suffered. Shops went out of business, buildings were destroyed, and the neighborhood became rife with flophouses, missions, and panhandlers. This atmosphere continued to cement the idea of Skid Row as a dangerous and seedy place.

Fortunately, the neighborhood reclaimed its history, cleaned up the area, and became Seattle's first historic district.

After more than a century of transformation, Pioneer Square, Seattle's former Skid Row, is home to art galleries, shops, restaurants, and entertainment venues.

A MIGHTY WOMAN WITH A TORCH

Where is the statue of liberty found?

Standing only seven and a half feet tall, West Seattle's Lady Liberty is a fraction of the size of the original in New York's harbor. She's a replica of the real one and not even an accurate replica, but she still serves as a patriotic gathering place for the community. Runners, volleyball players, and beach explorers all slow down a moment to give a nod to what she represents.

Lady Liberty arrived in Seattle in 1952, donated to the city by the Boy Scouts. The statue was installed in West Seattle, not far from where the Denny Party initially landed and first named the settlement New York Alki.

The statue has been bruised and battered over the years. She's been knocked off her pedestal, had her arm ripped off, had her crown stolen, and been the victim of vandalism. She hadn't aged well either, so it was no surprise when it was time for a facelift.

In 2006, Lady Liberty got a remake that included an upgrade to bronze and a new pedestal. She got a coat of green copper paint, and the following year was back in residence on Alki. Her home needed an update next, and a fundraising campaign sold engraved bricks to individuals and businesses. With great community pride, the new statue and plaza were dedicated in 2008.

SEATTLE'S LADY LIBERTY

WHAT: Public art

WHERE: Statue of Liberty Plaza, Alki Beach

COST: Free

PRO TIP: The base of the statue has become a memorial site for poignant occasions, most recently the death of Justice Ruth Bader Ginsburg.

Seattle's version of the Statue of Liberty in West Seattle

The Statue of Liberty has seen a lot over the years. She's been a backdrop for protests and rallies. She has been a community gathering place during times of grief. And while Elliott Bay is not New York Harbor, and Alki Beach does not attract millions of visitors each year, Seattle's Lady Liberty is still meaningful. She commemorates the city's founding and stands guard over visitors to her beach.

A time capsule discovered in the base of the statue contained a miniature Statue of Liberty. Its arm had been ripped off, eerily similar to the larger one.

ICKY STICKY

Where can you find a wall of gum?

Chewing gum. On the wall. That's what the Seattle Gum Wall is all about. It might seem like it's more complicated than that, but that's all it is—a wall full of chewing gum accumulated over nearly a decade.

The Gum Wall is located in Post Alley at the Pike Place Market, right outside the Market Theater. The gum first made its appearance in 1993 when theater patrons began sticking gum on the wall and then sticking a coin in the gum while queuing up for their tickets and admission. Weeks went by, and everyone kept sticking gum to the wall. On a couple of occasions, the market told the theater to remove the gum and clean off the wall. They did. But the gum kept coming back.

Somewhere amid all the scraping and cleaning, the Gum Wall took on a life of its own until finally, in 1999, Pike Place Market officials gave up and declared the Gum Wall an official tourist attraction. The tradition of sticking chewing gum to the wall continued, and the market stepped out of the way.

Sugar in the gum caused erosion of the bricks, and after 20 years left unattended, the wall needed scrubbing as part of routine maintenance. Over 2,350 pounds of gum was removed,

GUM WALL

WHAT: Interactive public art

WHERE: 1428 Post Alley

COST: Free

PRO TIP: If you head to the Gum Wall for your photo op, be sure not to lean back or touch the wall.

A wall of gum in Post Alley

more than 50 pieces of gum per brick. Immediately after the scrubbing, gum returned.

It's become a bit of a tourist attraction, whether for the sheer quirkiness of the wall or because some people consider it a type of interactive public art. If you think this all sounds gross and unsanitary, you're right. But if you're walking around the market on a sunny weekend, it wouldn't be unusual to see a smiling bride and groom posing for photos.

The Gum Wall is second on the list of the most unsanitary attractions, right behind the Blarney Stone.

RINGY DINGY

Where are the vintage telephones?

There was a time when our words made their way across the country accompanied by a string of clicks, rattles, and pings. Every phone call made through switching equipment felt like a technological miracle, and in many ways, it was. Connections Museum Seattle (originally called the Vintage Telephone Equipment Museum) shares these milestones of the telecommunications industry's heritage with everyone who stops by.

At the advent of the digital revolution, the Connections Museum founders were aware that newer technology would soon replace older electro-mechanical telephone technology. To preserve as much as they could, they occupied a former switching station and, through their contacts, started amassing pieces of switching equipment. A replica of the first phone used by Alexander Graham Bell provides a starting point to put the displays into some sense of a timeline.

Phones and other communication equipment from the 20th century were added to the museum, supplementing the more massive telecommunication relics. Some of the favorite vintage pieces include teletype machines, reel-to-reel tape recorders, PBX boards, and payphones. An original camera that KING 5 News used during the late '50s looks cumbersome compared to what news teams shoot

CONNECTIONS MUSEUM SEATTLE

WHAT: Specialty museum dedicated to all things telephony

WHERE: 7000 E. Marginal Way S.

COST: Suggested donation of $5

PRO TIP: Listen to the voice of the Time Lady. A phone customer could call for the precise time, and actress Jane Barbe's voice would respond and accurately give the time in 15-second increments.

Vintage telephone at the Connections Museum Seattle

with today. And while the World's Fair was correct in its prediction of video phones, the current iteration of cell phone products was beyond what anyone thought would be possible.

Some displays are well-curated with annotations. Others look like a hodge-podge of wires and cable—because that's what used to make the whole system work. The museum staff is all volunteers, giving their time because they have an interest in and appreciation for telephony, and are quick to share their knowledge with facts and stories and by pointing out technical documentation.

Connections is located on the second (partial) and third floor of a current telephone engineering station. The station is fully computerized and rarely has staff on site. It's a contrast with the museum displays of equipment that required round-the-clock staffing and maintenance. We've come a long way.

The Connections Museum Seattle offers visitors a look at the impact the telecommunications industry has had on society and culture.

FINS OF NAVAL HISTORY

Where can you find submarine fins?

The property occupied by Magnuson Park is where Sand Point Naval Air Station was located during the Cold War. Artist John T. Young was called upon to find a use for fin-like diving planes from decommissioned US Navy nuclear submarines. He developed the concept for Fin Art, dedicated in 1998, preserving military history in multiple ways.

The larger-than-life installation is made of 22 ebony fins protruding out of the earth. The fins range from 4 to 12 feet tall, and each weighs about 10,000 pounds. Since the fins are made of high-tensile, military-grade steel, they are solid and virtually indestructible. Arranged in an irregular pattern over a space of about 500 feet, they require little upkeep or maintenance. While the fins came from nuclear submarines, rest assured they are free of toxic substances and completely inert.

The sculpture was a gift to Seattle. Generous donations from local businesses, agencies, and individuals made the art installation possible. Even the US Navy contributed to the project.

> ### FIN ART
>
> **WHAT:** Public art
>
> **WHERE:** Magnuson Park, 7400 Sand Point Way NE
>
> **COST:** Free
>
> **PRO TIP:** Allow time to enjoy the path that follows the shoreline of Lake Washington.

Set on the west shore of Lake Washington, *Fin Art* resembles a pod of orca swimming through the ocean.

Top: *Fins from nuclear submarines have been turned into public art in Magnuson Park.*
Bottom: *Enjoy a peaceful walk along the Lake Washington shoreline.*

As is the case with most art, Seattle's *Fin Art* represents different things to different people. Those with an affinity for whales or submarines usually see it as a simple, straightforward art piece on the topic. Others interpret it as a display of how used goods can be recycled into public art. For others, it speaks to the idea of turning wartime relics into art that closes the door to a military past.

TEEMING WITH ELECTRICITY

Where does electricity come from?

A substation usually brings to mind a large, bleak, gray space covered in warning signs. They are utilitarian in design and not meant to be beautiful. Local architecture firm NBBJ challenged that stereotype when designing the new substation on Denny Way.

When Seattle City Light set out to build the substation, they didn't envision it as a city icon. The city simply needed a vacant area in which to build a plain-old junky-looking station. The city's Design Commission had different ideas, though, and required public benefits to be included in the design.

Initially, the station was to be entirely underground with a public park right on top of it, but the concept had too many logistical problems. Instead, an alternative design called for an elevated pedestrian walkway surrounding the substation edges, with angled walls to make space for public amenities.

The finished substation covers a city block and is ADA accessible. It can meet all the city's present and future electrical needs while simultaneously being a symbol of pride for the community. The state-of-the-art structure features a gently sloped walkway with peepholes that enable pedestrians to look into the substation. Don't even think about climbing for a closer look—the camera and sensors set off an alarm to detect trespassers.

The substation has a small park, a meeting space, an exhibit hall, a small theater, and an Energy Inspiration Center. Public art

The Denny Substation is a recreational hub that powers its neighborhood, literally and figuratively.

Seattle City Light's Denny Substation covers a city block.

DENNY SUBSTATION

WHAT: Public space

WHERE: 1250 Denny Way

COST: Free

PRO TIP: Bring your dog and enjoy the off-leash area.

also shines, including a sound art installation projecting rushing water sounds to simulate hydroelectric facility noises. The station also includes on-site solar power, a heat recovery system, and other sustainability features.

LET'S GET (META) PHYSICAL

Where are research materials on UFOs and alternative theories of the universe?

Tucked away beneath the Kress Building in Ballard, the Seattle Metaphysical Library isn't the easiest to spot, but that only adds to its allure. Locating this elusive library is a fitting way to start your mystical journey into the metaphysical and unusual. The lease doesn't permit signage, but a small sandwich board is out front when the library is open.

Legally registered as the As-You-Like-It Library, it has been around for about half a century, catering to its niche users' needs. It was first set up at the Pike Place Market by three retired teachers who wanted to share their unusual interests with the community. Over time and following numerous relocations, the collection has grown to a staggering assortment of over 16,000 books, magazines, videos, and pieces of digital content across 77 esoteric categories.

Whether it's career-killing topics or merely the unconventional and contrarian, these are books you won't find elsewhere. The library is well known for its collections of materials on alternative health, UFOs, and conspiracy theories, providing the most in-depth information in Seattle. Special events include tarot

SEATTLE METAPHYSICAL LIBRARY

WHAT: Specialty library

WHERE: 2220 NW Market St., #L-05

COST: Membership is required to check out books: $25 per year to check out one book at a time; $50 per year to check out three books. Free to do research on-site.

PRO TIP: The library has one of the largest collections of books on Dianetics outside of Scientology libraries.

Research in the stacks at the Seattle Metaphysical Library in Ballard

readings, book club discussion groups, guest speakers, and group trips. And while this is a library, not a bookstore, items such as tarot cards, duplicate books, and icons are occasionally for sale.

Library hours are irregular as it's staffed entirely by volunteers. It's best to call before paying a visit.

The Seattle Metaphysical Library is a space for reading and research as well as a safe haven to connect with others who share similar interests.

BIG SHOES TO FILL

Where are large-sized shoes found?

In old-style traveling carnivals, the thrill acts, freak shows, and oddity exhibits were meant to be recreational detours from the carousels and Ferris wheels. Although undoubtedly inspired by circus sideshows, the Giant Shoe Museum at the Pike Place Market is the main attraction, albeit a small one. Despite occupying only one wall, the museum attracts intrigued visitors interested in what lies behind the stereoscope viewer.

Located on a lower level at the market, the wall has a loud boardwalk-style design. Despite its carnie look, it's easy to walk past it. It's billed as a museum, but it is just a display. Once you find it, a couple of quarters is all you need to take a peep. The curtains move aside to reveal founder Danny Eskenazi's giant-shoe collection. You'll see specialties like the world's largest shoe, authentic clown shoes, and a curious sign that offers $1,000 for a Robert Wadlow shoe.

Standing 8'11", Robert Wadlow was the tallest man in the world and the reason Eskenazi became obsessed with giant shoes in the first place. When Eskenazi learned that his grandfather had once owned one of Wadlow's shoes but that it had gotten lost during a move, he began trying to locate it. The shoe was never found, but the sign and the reward remain. Eskenazi amassed a collection of giant shoes during his search, and some of them are displayed at the Giant Shoe Museum today.

Interest in sideshows declined over the years as it became easier and more affordable to see the world's weirdest attractions

---

Standing 8'11", Robert Wadlow was the tallest man in the world and wore a size 37AA shoe.

The Big Shoe Museum peep show is on the Pike Place Market's lower level.

right from the comfort of our homes. Moreover, changes in public opinion made sideshows fall into disrepute—so much so that even the more innocuous ones ended in oblivion. It's curious, then, that the Giant Shoe Museum holds a certain nostalgic appeal today.

GIANT SHOE MUSEUM

WHAT: Peep show of shoes

WHERE: 1501 Pike Pl., #424

COST: Peep shows are 25 and 50 cents.

PRO TIP: A $1,000 bounty is offered to anyone finding the shoes of Robert Wadlow, who holds the record as the tallest man who ever lived.

VLADIMIR LENIN LIVES IN SEATTLE

What's a Russian revolutionary doing in Seattle?

Former Communist leader Vladimir Lenin died in 1924 and his body is embalmed and on permanent display in a mausoleum in Red Square in Moscow, Russia. He was moody and volatile, a violent zealot with little sense of humor. In contrast, the Vladimir Lenin in Seattle is a 16-foot bronze statue that has worn a tutu, carried political signs, and been adorned with Christmas lights (red of course). This Lenin has a sense of humor and style.

After the 1989 Velvet Revolution, Czechoslovakia removed all Communist icons from public view, and as a result the statue of Lenin wound up in a scrapyard. Issaquah resident Lewis E. Carpenter discovered the statue, recognized its artistic value, and decided to buy it. The purchase price was $13,000. By the time the statue arrived in Seattle, though, that price had crept up to $40,000, and Carpenter mortgaged his home to pay for it.

In 1993, Lenin's statue arrived in Issaquah in three pieces. Six months later, and before Carpenter could make arrangements to display the statue, he was killed in a car accident. His family decided to sell the pieces to a local foundry, melt the parts, and create something new and less controversial. Instead, the Fremont Chamber of Commerce agreed to display the statue, holding it in trust until a buyer could be found.

There have been multiple attempts to have the statue removed. It's easy to see how a giant statue of a Communist revolutionary

WELL-DRESSED LENIN

WHAT: Public art

WHERE: 3526 Fremont Pl. N., Fremont

COST: Free

PRO TIP: The eight-ton bronze statue of Lenin is still for sale. The last known asking price was $250,000.

A bronze statue of Lenin is located in Fremont.

could offend sensibilities. There are several explanations as to why Lenin remains. Whether it's a simple joke or an ironic reminder that the United States survived, and the USSR did not, art has trumped politics so far.

The statue of Lenin remains in Fremont, erected on private property at the edge of a parking lot. Community members keep him in sartorial splendor, providing clothing and accessories to coordinate with holidays and community events. The Fremont Chamber of Commerce still holds the Lenin statue in trust, waiting for a buyer to be found.

Fremont kicks off the holiday season with the annual Lenin Lighting, draping the statue with Christmas lights.

CANDY MAKING HISTORY

What candy is Tacoma known for?

In the early 1900s, Tacoma, Washington, was the center of US candy making. The Pacific Northwest weather was mild enough to be conducive to chocolate making, and Tacoma had direct access to the railroads and ships that moved products around the country and world. There were more than 50 candy makers in Tacoma at one point, including the likes of Frank C. Mars, the maker of the Milky Way, 3 Musketeers, and Snickers bars.

Mars left before he found success, but one company that stuck it out and thrived is Brown & Haley. Its path to candy fame began in 1908, when candy maker Harry Brown met salesman J. C. Haley at their local church. Over the next five years, their friendship grew, and eventually they decided to start the Oriole Candy Company together. They hit the ground running with the success of their first creation, the Mount Tacoma Bar, today known as the Mountain Bar. As World War I brought soldiers practically to the company's doorstep at nearby Fort Lewis, Oriole Candy changed its name to Brown & Haley.

After the war, as sales slowed, Brown & Haley knew it was time to pivot. They came up with the idea to cut toffee into small logs, preventing them from sticking together and creating a bite-sized candy. The chocolate and almond-coated

ALMOND ROCA

WHAT: Factory store

WHERE: 110 E. 26th St., Tacoma

COST: $4.99 for a five-ounce stand-up box of the original Almond Roca

PRO TIP: Almond Roca is gluten-free.

Brown & Haley, maker of Almond Roca, is the largest exporter of gift candy in America.

Left: *The Almond Roca factory store is in Tacoma and is shaped like a candy container.* Below: *Almond Roca is gluten-free.*

sweet treat was introduced to the public in 1923, and a local librarian called it Roca, which means "rock" in Spanish. Since most almonds came from Spain during that time, it made perfect sense, and the name stuck.

The company designed its now-famous pink tin box, which made Almond Roca export-ready. In the tin box, the candy stayed fresh longer, and it became known as "the candy that travels." Families sent tins to soldiers stationed abroad during World War II. Sir Edmund Hillary took some along on an ascent of Mt. Everest. Soon the gold foil–wrapped bites in the pink tin were well known around the world.

Because of Brown & Haley's convenient location near the Port of Tacoma, it was well placed for exportation. It first developed partnerships in Japan and China, expanding to the 63 countries it exports to today. Exports make up 40 percent of company sales, proving candy that travels is big business. Christmas is the top Almond Roca selling season, followed by Chinese New Year and Valentine's Day.

A factory store in Tacoma, built in the shape of a candy box, offers all the Brown & Haley candy at a reduced price.

45

BRUCE LEE'S FAVORITE RESTAURANT

What's the oldest Chinese restaurant in Seattle?

Located on one of the original blocks in the International District, Tai Tung is the oldest Chinese restaurant in Seattle and has served customers for five generations. Some of those customers were children when they first visited and now bring their grandchildren to experience the Chan family food and enjoy its history.

The restaurant seems frozen in time. Owner Harry Chan takes great pride that almost everything, from the counter and cash register to the old wooden doors and menu, is just as it always has been.

TAI TUNG RESTAURANT

WHAT: Restaurant

WHERE: 655 S. King St. (International District)

COST: Entrees range from $13 to $16.

PRO TIP: Actor and martial artist Bruce Lee's favorite dishes were oyster sauce beef and garlic shrimp.

When his grandfather opened the restaurant in 1935, it quickly became a favorite among the single migrant workers from Asia. Family members of many of the men who worked at Tai Tung during those early years have remained fiercely loyal to the restaurant. College students, late-night revelers, and swing shift workers took advantage of extended hours—at one time, the restaurant was open until 3:45 a.m. Tai Tung became a retro icon in the International District, thanks to its good food, fortuitous popularity, and family commitment to quality standards.

From the opening of its doors, Tai Tung has had chop suey on the menu. The dish reached peak popularity in the '50s and '60s, and the restaurant had a flashing neon sign that said "Chop Suey." During a remodel in the late '60s, the first and only remodel the

Left: *Bruce Lee and his son, Brandon, are buried in Lake View Cemetery.* Inset: *The chop suey sign that hangs outside of Tai Tung in the International District.*

restaurant has gone through, the sign was tossed aside. Officially, the neon was lost or discarded. Unofficially, however, many wonder whether the sign became politicized, inadvertently promoting the racist sentiment that had come to be associated with the term "chop suey."

Chop suey is a term for Chinese-American cuisine known for using ingredients that are local and readily available. It was eating local before eating local became a marketing phrase. When the new sign, a replica of the original, was hung in 2017, it was like coming full circle back to the way things were. The way things are meant to stay. At least at Tai Tung.

Martial artist Bruce Lee moved to Seattle in 1959 to finish high school and attend the University of Washington. He worked in a Chinese restaurant in the International District.

CRANES FOR PEACE

What is the significance of origami cranes?

Floyd Schmoe was a Seattle marine biologist, park ranger, and college professor. He was also a pacifist and peace activist.

During World War II, he worked with British Quakers to help thousands of Jews escape from Germany. He was vigorous in his opposition to Executive Order No. 9066, which mandated that Japanese Americans be interned as a security risk. Schmoe looked after interned families' homes and property, which otherwise might have been seized or stolen. He lived in a barbed-wire internment camp in Idaho, providing support and services to interned families. And when the camps finally closed, Schmoe helped families find homes, reclaim their property, and restart their businesses. He deemed his actions to be essential to his abiding beliefs.

After World War II ended, Schmoe raised funds to start "Houses for Hiroshima." He spent five years in Japan, building homes to replace those destroyed by the atomic bomb.

SEATTLE PEACE PARK

WHAT: Public park and statue

WHERE: 802 NE 40th St.

COST: Free

PRO TIP: Floyd Schmoe was nominated for the Nobel Peace Prize three times, but he never won.

In 1988, Schmoe was awarded the Hiroshima Peace Prize, Japan's highest civilian honor, and made an honorary citizen of Japan.

The Peace Prize came with a small monetary award, and Schmoe used it to start a small park in Seattle. He found a strip of land near the University of Washington that had become overgrown with weeds and was covered with trash. He organized volunteers to clean up the area and persuaded the city to accept his Peace Park proposal.

Neighbors create origami cranes in memory of Sadako Sasaki.

The small park needed a statue. Artist Daryl Smith created a bronze statue of Sadako Sasaki, a Japanese girl who survived the Hiroshima bombing but died of leukemia from radiation at age 12. While hospitalized, she set a goal to make 1,000 paper cranes before she died. Since then, paper cranes have become international symbols of peace.

Seattle's Peace Park was dedicated on August 6, 1990, the 45th anniversary of the Hiroshima bombing. For the remaining 10 years of his life, Schmoe took an active part in caring for the park. He died at the age of 105. Today hundreds of children visit the unassuming little park each year to drape Sasaki in wreaths of paper cranes.

While it may look like nothing more than a tiny wedge of green space, the Peace Park has a rich history of hope.

THE HAUNTED CASTLE

Are there ghosts in Georgetown?

The cheerful, pumpkin-orange exterior of the 100-year old Georgetown Castle does an excellent job of concealing its rather grisly past. Lynda Bazan and her son, Micah Schlede, the current owners of the castle, made that a top priority when they took on the mammoth task of restoring and renovating it in 2004. Only upon closer inspection will you find a metal placard detailing the macabre history of the mansion.

It all started in 1902, when Peter Gessner, a gambler and blackjack dealer, decided to build a home for his wife, Lizzie. The Castle, as it later came to be known, was built in a classic Queen Anne style, complete with its projecting gables and turrets. This lovely gesture fell flat, as Lizzie began an affair with a local chicken farmer and left Gessner before the house was completed.

Gessner's woes continued when the police raided his gambling and brothel business. Since the mansion was empty, he moved his business there. A year later, Gessner died under suspicious circumstances. Although his death was considered suicide from drinking carbolic acid, there were plenty of rumors that foul play was involved. Meanwhile, Lizzie and the chicken farmer got married, moved into the Castle, and closed down the illicit businesses. It didn't take long for stories to circulate that Gessner had never left his home and that his ghost remained.

It proved difficult for the Georgetown Castle to escape its shame, and it went through a series of sketchy incarnations as a brothel,

---

GEORGETOWN CASTLE

WHAT: Private residence

WHERE: 6420 Carleton Ave. S.

COST: Free

PRO TIP: The Central Bar where Peter Gessner ran his gambling operations was the forerunner of the current Central Saloon located in Pioneer Square.

speakeasy, and gentlemen's club. Eventually it was converted to a respectable boarding house, and in the 1970s it housed Boeing workers.

Through the decades, the mansion has been a hotbed for paranormal activity. The reported activity includes the sighting of a woman with dark hair, believed to be a former employee of the brothel; sounds of men fighting; and noises believed to be related to a child's death.

The Georgetown Castle's present owners seem to have succeeded in injecting new life into their home—and not the paranormal type. The front yard is lush and green, and from the exterior the house looks lovingly maintained and peaceful. Let's hope the spirits, too, have found peace.

Paranormal experts have investigated Georgetown Castle and confirm there is unexplained activity.

DON'T FORGET TO VISIT YOUR MUMMY

Where can you find a mummy?

During the Civil War era, a wee third-grader named Joseph Standley was rewarded with a book called *Wonders of Nature* for having the neatest desk in his class. It piqued his curiosity, and he began amassing all the odd things he could find. Later, as a young man living in Denver, he tacked his trinkets to the walls of the grocery store he owned. Soon there was no wall space left.

During the Klondike Gold Rush, Standley packed up his family and his things and moved to Seattle. He set up Ye Olde Curiosity Shop on the waterfront, and that's where his collection flourished for more than a century. Seattle was booming in 1889, with thousands of explorers passing through Standley's store to get to Alaska. He struck up some long-lasting connections with Native American and Alaskan traders during this time, and his store became known for its Indian artifacts. His collection became so large and expansive that he won a gold medal at the Alaska-Yukon-Pacific Exposition, attracting famous customers like Robert Ripley.

Four generations later, the store now has a souvenir section and Native American artwork. Arguably, though, the shop's biggest draw is its massive assortment of odd and rather grotesque curiosities that often overshadows the art. The staff loves sharing stories about their favorite items in the store.

Sylvester and his counterpart, Sylvia, are the store's resident mummies. Sylvester was found in the Gila Bend desert in Arizona in 1895. He is one of the best-preserved mummies to exist and has been subjected to modern forensics and studied by National Geographic. It is believed that mummification occurred because

The mummies at Ye Olde Curiosity Shop have been authenticated by modern forensics.

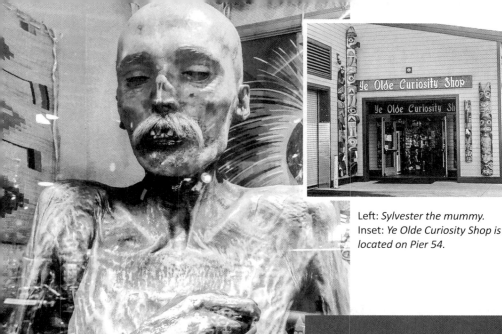

Left: *Sylvester the mummy.*
Inset: *Ye Olde Curiosity Shop is located on Pier 54.*

SYLVIA & SYLVESTER

WHAT: Art and curiosity store

WHERE: 1001 Alaskan Way on Pier 54

COST: Free

PRO TIP: The shop has supplied museums with authentic Native American and Alaska Native art.

an embalmer injected arsenic-based fluid shortly after his death. Medical Ed, a cadaver head used as a dissection aid in the early 1900s, is another well-preserved specimen that's a shop favorite.

The walls and display cases at Ye Olde Curiosity Shop are crammed to the brim with odd bits and bobs. You'll find shrunken heads from Ecuador, a leprechaun's foot, oil paintings on pinheads, a 67-pound snail, the world's smallest safety pin, and a coin that weighs in at 6 pounds. There are taxidermied animals of all sorts, including a two-headed duckling and a duck-billed platypus. Hanging from the ceiling is a dusty Fiji mermaid, fabled to have been caught on the shores of Duckabush.

Despite all the items up for viewing, the most priceless thing you may find might be what Standley found all those years ago in his third-grade class—a renewed curiosity about the world and all the strange things it has to offer.

GET YOUR EXERCISE

Where is the longest stairway in Seattle?

The Howe Street Stairs, also known as the East Howe Steps, are Seattle's longest continuous stairway. How long? With 388 successive steps and 160 feet of elevation, the Howe Street Stairs are a stairway to fitness that connects the Capitol Hill and Eastlake neighborhoods. The stairs' endpoints are at Eastlake Avenue and Howe Street. In between are 13 flights of stairs broken up by streets and landings.

The stairs were constructed in 1911 to connect two different lines of Seattle's streetcar system. They eased the difficulty of getting between the two lines because of Seattle's hills and topography. Eventually, the stairs became a connection between neighborhoods, both for social and business purposes, and they have remained in use long after the streetcars' demise.

Although the stairs were built to ease transportation, residents started to come to the stairs to run and get some exercise. After all, as your doctor or trainer may have told you, stair climbing is an excellent low-impact physical activity that can increase your heart rate, tone your legs, and burn body fat. Athletes often run stairs in their stadiums, and the Howe Street stairs approximate that experience.

The stairs are broad, and during less busy times families and friends can run together—side by side, if you run at the same speed. The stairs are well-used, though, often full of people commuting to work or getting in their workout. Hope for the best, but be prepared for crowds.

HOWE STREET STAIRS

WHAT: Public staircase

WHERE: 810 E. Howe St.

COST: Free

PRO TIP: The Blaine Staircase, which runs parallel to the stairs, is only 293 steps.

The Howe Street Stairs are used to commute between Eastlake and Capitol Hill.

The stairs traverse verdant backyards that are exceptionally beautiful in spring, when plants are in bloom, and provide shade during the summer months. If you are winded and need a rest, stopping to identify an attractive plant is always a good option.

Over the years, the Howe Street Stairs have turned into an outdoor recreation center that serves as an excellent alternative to boring cardio workouts at the gym. If you're not in tip-top shape, don't worry. You can take it slow, taking advantage of the landings to stop and rest for a moment.

The Howe Street Stairs pass through the I-5 Colonnade, a 7.5-acre park located beneath I-5.

A REACH FOR BIKE SAFETY

How does Seattle keep bikers safe?

The Dutch Reach is a simple practice that involves drivers exiting their car in a way that keeps cyclist safety in mind. Michael Charney, a 73-year-old Dutch activist, came up with a simple way to avoid doorings (opening a door into a cyclist) and accidents caused when a cyclist swerves to avoid a dooring. It's a simple behavioral change that saves lives.

Washington State adopted the Dutch Reach and in 2019 included it in the state's Driver Guide. Although Seattle promotes itself as one of the top bike-friendly cities in the United States, most drivers aren't aware of this simple safety procedure.

Here's how it works: After parking the car, check for traffic using the rear-view and side-view mirrors. To open the door, use the right hand to reach across the body toward the door. Reaching across like this forces the body to swivel and, in doing so, gives the driver a better look to see approaching cyclists. Open the door with the right hand, exit the car, and quickly close the door.

Taken a step further, passengers should follow the same example, reversing the process and opening the door with the left hand. This can help check for cyclists as well as passengers.

THE DUTCH REACH

WHAT: Safety protocol

WHERE: Everywhere

COST: Free

PRO TIP: Attach a brightly colored ribbon or band to the car door as a reminder to use your far hand to open the door.

As the name suggests, the Dutch Reach was pioneered in the Netherlands, one of the most bike-friendly countries in the world.

to open door
USE FAR HAND

dutchreach.org   NM-18

The Dutch Reach slows down the process of opening a car door for a few precious seconds. Those seconds not only protect cyclists and pedestrians but also help reduce vehicular damage. It can be challenging to learn a new habit, but following the Dutch Reach requires only a simple behavior change and can save lives.

WHAT A VIEW

Where is the best view of Seattle?

Located on Queen Anne Hill's south slope, Kerry Park is a small public park that runs along West Highland Drive between Second and Third avenues west. The upper edge of the park offers some of the best views of the Seattle skyline as you face south toward the city. You'll often see this view published in print and online and as a green-screen backdrop for Seattle television news and talk shows.

Kerry Park covers 1.26 acres. It was named after Albert Kerry, a Northwest lumberman known for his contributions to the city. He donated the land on which the park now stands. A stairway on the west end of the park leads to a smaller park called Bayview-Kinnear Park, with a small playground. Although it is a separate park, it is virtually indistinguishable from Kerry Park. The average visitor won't know the difference between the two parks. It will all be seen as one.

VIEW FROM KERRY PARK

WHAT: Park

WHERE: West Highland Drive, between Second and Third avenues west

COST: Free

PRO TIP: Sunset is considered the best time of day for stunning city photos.

A 15-foot-high steel sculpture, known as *Changing Form*, is located at the center of the park. Artist Doris Totten Chase created a sculpture of large circles and ellipses on the sides of two stacked hollow cubes. It's a popular play area for children, and unlike with some art, climbing on this sculpture is perfectly acceptable. It is also frequently used by photographers as a frame of the skyline. While the park is popular with families in the neighborhood, it has become even more popular, famous even, because of the photo opportunities it offers.

The best views of Seattle can be captured from Kerry Park on Queen Anne Hill.

Although Kerry Park is a great place to visit irrespective of time or season, sunset and its afterglow offer the most beautiful views from the park. The night sky aglow with city lights and the ferries gliding across Puget Sound create a popular scene for Seattle photos. Late afternoon and sunset are also popular times for outdoor wedding ceremonies and romantic dates.

If you've seen a sweeping skyline photo that includes the Space Needle, downtown, and Elliott Bay, there's an excellent chance that it was taken from Kerry Park.

CAN YOU FIND THE TIME

What's with all the street clocks?

Street clocks, also called pedestal clocks, first made their appearance in America in the 1800s, around the same time the railroad came. Scheduled trains meant that passengers needed to be at train stations on time, and not everyone carried personal timepieces. Soon enough, community clocks began showing up on every corner. The trend first cropped up in the east, but once jewelers and other merchants realized it could be profitable, the trend—and the trains—headed west.

By the end of the 1800s, Seattle boasted 24 post clocks in its cityscape, earning it the title "City of Clocks."

Jewelry merchants co-opted the street clock because they could put their store names on the clock faces. It became a way to work around laws that prohibited commercial signage on sidewalks. It also was an excellent way to market their jewelry business, and by the 1920s it was commonplace for jewelers to own and maintain giant clocks. Many of these opulent pieces of street furniture have survived through the years and can still be seen in Seattle's downtown area today.

By the mid-20th century, almost everyone owned a wristwatch, and the preferred mode of advertising became neon signs, making

CLOCK WALK

WHAT: Clocks

WHERE: All over downtown. See clock map for details: zombiezodiac.com/rob/ped/clock/map.htm.

COST: Free

PRO TIP: Most clocks were painted a dark green color, giving rise to the color name "street clock green."

The typical Seattle street clock stands 15 feet high and incorporates a pedestal base and column.

Top: *A question mark–shaped clock is on the corner of Fifth Avenue and Pine Street.* Inset: *The King Street Station tower clock.*

street clocks go from ubiquitous to obsolete. In recent years, however, there has been a revived interest in these clocks as historical monuments. Rob Ketcherside, a local historian, put together the Seattle Clock Walk to make it easier to find and visit them.

Seattle's Board of Public Works began efforts to remove the street clocks in the 1950s, citing an impingement on "pedestrian circulation." Clock owners and enthusiasts pushed through a compromise plan that allowed street clocks conditioned on the owners keeping them running and clean.

The clock compromise resulted in Seattle having one of the country's largest historic street clock collections. New timepieces continued to be added over the years, and unfortunately some classic ones have been lost. Perennial local favorites include the austere Ben Bridge Jeweler's clock, the welcoming Pike Place Market clock, and the tower clock on the King Street Station.

A SMALL AND SPITEFUL HOUSE

Where can you find a spite house?

The Montlake Spite House is an 860-square-foot wedge-shaped house built in 1925. A spite house is a building constructed or modified to hurt or irritate neighbors. The reason for the spite can vary—everything from blocking a view, blocking access, or sometimes just being a thorn in someone's side—but it's a deliberate choice to make a statement.

Two popular theories explain the construction of this spite house. The first is that a division of assets in an ugly divorce resulted in the husband being awarded the family home and the wife getting a small section of the property. As an act of revenge, the wife built a small and unusually shaped house that fit the tiny piece of property awarded to her.

The second theory suggests that a neighbor approached a landowner to negotiate using the tiny bit of land to grow a garden. The owner was so offended by what he felt was an unfair offer that he decided to build a home on the property and block the neighbor's view.

The house's interior is interesting and unusual—the space packs in many practical design elements to create luxurious small-space living. There are two bedrooms, two living rooms, two bathrooms, a kitchen, a basement, a garage, and a nice yard. The main entrance flows into a staircase that leads to a 9-by-14-foot living room. The upper floor also has a small dining corner. At its widest

Although spite houses are currently not permitted under Seattle housing codes, the regulation came along after the Montlake Spite House was built.

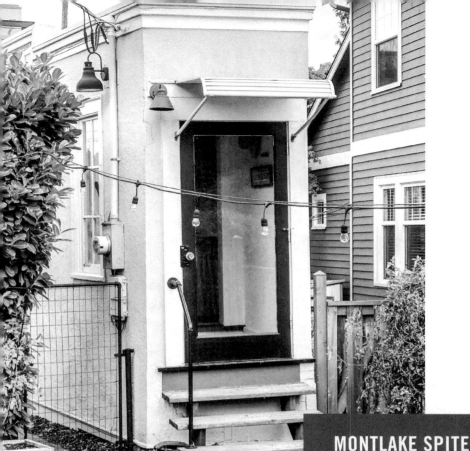

This spite house is located in the Montlake neighborhood.

MONTLAKE SPITE HOUSE

WHAT: Private home

WHERE: 2022 24th Ave. E.

COST: Free to walk by, considerably more if you want to buy it

PRO TIP: While the house may look strange and impractical, it is surprisingly valued at over half a million dollars.

point in the master bedroom, the house is 15 feet wide. At its narrowest, a small mudroom adjacent to the kitchen, it is 55 inches wide.

The residence has a fenced backyard with room for a patio, flower planters, and a seating area. The front yard, which faces a heavily trafficked street, has a mature hedge to block out noise and provide privacy. The property was last sold in 2016 for around $500,000.

IT'S ELECTRIFYING

Where did Seattle's electricity come from?

The Georgetown Steam Plant represents technological advancements that paved the way for the electrification of America's cities. It houses two vertical Curtis turbines manufactured by General Electric in 1907.

The Curtis turbines were vertical steam turbo-generators that were more efficient than the previously used reciprocating steam engine. This technology meant the steam plant could keep up with the increased demand for electricity in the Seattle area. The city needed more and more electricity to power streetcar and rail lines and provide electricity for homes and businesses.

Eventually hydropower began to outperform steam power, and the steam plant was forced into retirement. Seattle City Light has owned the plant since 1951. The plant last produced electricity in 1953, when water in the dam reservoirs was perilously low. It was decommissioned and permanently retired in 1977.

Founded in 1995, the Georgetown Powerplant Museum, in partnership with City Light, set out to restore and maintain the plant. The turbines represent some of the last remaining in existence. Along with the plant, several smaller steam engines and the collection of vintage machine tools have helped to land it on the National Historic Landmark list.

The list of needed repairs and improvements is lengthy. And expensive. In the meantime, limited public tours are offered. The

Although unused for nearly 70 years, the Georgetown Steam Plant remains an archetypal landmark that connects Seattle with its engineering history.

Top: *The Georgetown Steam Plant is situated adjacent to runways at King County Airport.* Bottom: *Industrial chic and utility are united inside the Georgetown Steam Plant.*

plant's architecture—once practical but now edgy industrial chic—has been used as a setting for concerts, plays, special events, and even zombie photo shoots.

The Georgetown Steam Plant stands as an example of how quickly technology changes life, and of how quickly something new and cutting edge can become obsolete.

THESE BOOTS AREN'T MADE FOR WALKING

Where can you see oversized western wear?

The Hat 'n' Boots at Oxbow Park took 15 minutes to conceptualize and 15 years to save. At least that's how long artist Lewis Nasmyth says it took him to develop the idea. Nasmyth was asked to design a gas station for a new Western-themed shopping center in the Georgetown neighborhood. The main requirement was that it be flashy enough to catch the attention of passersby.

The design featured a massive cowboy hat, 44 feet in diameter, that covered the gas station office, and a pair of cowboy boots, 22 feet tall, that housed the restrooms. After a year of careful design and execution, Hat 'n' Boots was complete, and the Premium Tex Gas Station (Texaco) opened for business in 1954 with service attendants dressed in cowboy outfits. The swanky new Western-themed gas station was an immediate hit.

Longtime Georgetown residents remember the excitement of visiting the gas station. With Hat 'n' Boots as a cornerstone attraction, Tex Gas Station became the state's top-selling gas station.

Unfortunately, the success was short-lived. Financial stress took its toll, and the opening of Interstate 5 siphoned traffic away from the neighborhood. Hat 'n' Boots foundered, eventually going out of business. Everyone seemed to forget about the once-thriving establishment, and bit by bit it went from icon to eyesore.

For 15 sorry years, Hat 'n' Boots was a blight in the neighborhood until plans were made to tear it down. This threat

According to rumor, Elvis Presley supposedly stopped by Hat 'n' Boots while in town for Seattle's 1962 World's Fair.

A giant hat and boots are an attraction at Oxbow Park.

HAT 'N' BOOTS

WHAT: Public park

WHERE: 6430 Corson Ave. S.

COST: Free

PRO TIP: Restrooms are located in the boots.

galvanized the community, and residents took to the streets in their Western garb to protest. Eventually the site was purchased from the City of Seattle for $1. It took community fundraising of a couple hundred thousand more to save Hat 'n' Boots and move it to a new location four blocks away.

After a long and arduous renovation process, the community finally restored the Hat 'n' Boots to its former glory in 2010. It now serves as a central attraction in a neighborhood park and community garden. These boots—and hat—aren't going anywhere.

A LITERARY CITY

Why was Seattle chosen as a UNESCO City of Literature?

In October 2017, the United Nations Educational, Scientific and Cultural Organization (UNESCO) chose Seattle as its 28th City of Literature. There are only 39 Cities of Literature representing 28 different countries, so Seattle is in outstanding company. It is only the second City of Literature in the United States. The other is Iowa City.

To be chosen as a City of Literature, a city submits bids that are reviewed by UNESCO to determine the role of literature in the cities. The program also looks at the number of literary events and libraries in a city and how it promotes a reading culture.

Seattle was chosen as a City of Literature in large part due to its long-standing reading culture and support of writers and literary events. The city has dozens of independent bookstores that span diverse cultural heritages and interests and manage to co-exist and thrive in a city that is also home to Amazon.

The Seattle Public Library system, established in 1890, promotes reading and related events throughout the city. The flagship of the library system is the Central Library located downtown, 11 stories of glass and steel. The building's striking architecture landed it on the American Institute of Architects' list of Americans' 150 favorite structures in the United States, coming in at 108. The library can hold up to a million and a half books and other materials. Twenty-six neighborhood branches and a mobile program round out the library system.

SEATTLE CENTRAL LIBRARY

WHAT: Library

WHERE: 1000 Fourth Ave.

COST: Free to use facilities. Checking out books requires a library card.

PRO TIP: Former Seattle librarian Nancy Pearl, founder of the Book Lust reading lists, has an action figure modeled after her.

Central Library is the flagship of the Seattle Public Library system.

Although the Central Library design is not without its critics, residents have embraced it. The building's use has more than doubled expectations and attracts visitors for more than traditional library services. The library is known for its community events programs, including literary and film events, classes, author events, reading challenges, and more. It also offers free Wi-Fi.

The Central Library offers group and self-guided tours. A visitor favorite is the Red Hall, located on the fourth floor. The walls and walkways are curved, and the walls are a deep red color. It's stark, intense, and often disorienting. The fourth floor is where most of the meeting rooms are located.

September is Library Card Sign-Up Month.

UNESCO's City of Literature program is a part of the Creative Cities Network. The network also has seven other creative fields, including design, film, media arts, and music.

PINUPS

Who was Bettie Page?

Bettie Mae Page was an American model famous for her pinup photos. As teenagers, Page and her sisters tried different makeup styles and hairdos, taking inspiration from favorite movie stars. These skills helped Page later in her career.

After moving to New York from California to pursue her acting career, Page met a photographer who believed she would make a good pinup model. Page worked with him to develop a portfolio that, as predicted, launched her career as a model.

Page had jet-black hair that fell just below her shoulders, signature bangs, and blue eyes. Her style, both in looks and costumes, was bold and exotic, outrageous for the era. Page was the January 1955 Playmate of the Month and worked for years as a model for adult magazines.

Then, nearly as quickly as she rose to fame, she dropped out of the public eye. The reasons were not entirely clear. Rumors circulated that she retired because of Estes Kefauver's indecency hearings in Congress. Other stories related her retirement to finding religion, returning to school, or experiencing mental health issues.

In the 1980s, Page had a resurgence of fame, this time attracting legions of female fans. She became a symbol of female empowerment, ushering in an era of sex-positivity. More photos appeared, and biographies were published. Page gave interviews and made public appearances, and despite her bouts of mental health problems and legal issues, she remained a popular figure until she died in 2008.

BETTIE PAGE HOUSE

WHAT: Mural on private home

WHERE: 743 NE 58th St.

COST: Free

PRO TIP: In 2016, the mural was expanded to include a 12-foot painting of Divine, a well-known drag queen and actor.

Bettie Page and Divine bigger than life.

A Ravenna homeowner who was a big Page fan asked an artist friend to paint a mural of Page on the side of the home. The mural, completed in 2006, portrays an 18-foot Page in black underclothes that highlight her curvy and attractive body. She is given some modesty by rain gutters strategically placed to obscure her breasts.

Since Page's appearance on the home, there have been complaints and vandalism. Page has endured.

The Bettie Page mural is visible from the 65th Street exit on I-5 northbound.

EYES ON YOU

Where can granite eyes be found?

Eye Benches I, II, and *III* are a group of granite sculptures by Louise Joséphine Bourgeois installed at the Olympic Sculpture Park. Bourgeois is a French American artist known for her large-scale sculptures and installation art, centered on heavy themes such as sexuality, death, family, and unconsciousness. Heavily influenced by surrealism, she tried to express the subconscious mind through her art. Bourgeois was actively sculpting up until she died in 2010 and was also known as a painter and a printmaker.

Bourgeois developed the Eye Benches series idea during the last few months of her life. Just as their names suggest, the Eye Benches look like giant eyes and come two to a set. Carved out of black Zimbabwe granite, two are functional seating— interactive art. The eyes appear to be continually observing the sky, mountains, and people, conveying a joy of people watching while also providing a practical spot for Sculpture Park visitors to sit for a while.

Besides the Eye Benches, Bourgeois created another sculpture called *Father and Son* specifically for the Sculpture Park. The

---

EYE BENCHES

WHAT: Public art

WHERE: Olympic Sculpture Park, 2901 Western Ave.

COST: Free

PRO TIP: A free guide to the Sculpture Park can be picked up at SAM or downloaded from the museum website. It will save lots of time.

The nine-acre Olympic Sculpture Park, operated by the Seattle Art Museum (SAM), has sculptures and playful installations.

Top: *A pair of eyes by sculptor Louise Joséphine Bourgeois at Olympic Sculpture Park.* Inset: *Eye Bench close up.*

sculpture portrays a father and a son facing each other with arms outstretched and is made out of stainless steel, aluminum, water, and bronze. It represents the various phases in the relationship between a father and a son.

The Sculpture Park is interactive art at its finest. Touching, sitting, and climbing are generally permissible, making it an excellent family-friendly destination. It is also dog-friendly (on leashes).

POOH ON POO

Where's the best fertilizer for the garden?

Woodland Park Zoo is committed to its conservation efforts. So committed that they have got the animals in on the action. Although the hippos and rhinos contribute the most, the other non-primate herbivores also play an indispensable part in producing the 500-ton annual poo collection.

Since 1986, this animal waste has been collected and converted into high-quality compost. The compost, charmingly labeled Zoo Doo, is made from two main components: fresh manure and bedding material. Both are gathered from the animal enclosures and brought to the Zoo Doo Yard. The decomposition process takes three to four months and converts the smelly manure into rich, dirt-like compost. It's gardening gold.

The zoo makes two types of compost, Zoo Doo and Bedspread. The Zoo Doo compost helps serve as a primary source of nutrients while also providing the benefits of aeration and water retention to the soil. The Bedspread compost is more coarse and woody in texture. It also helps add to the soil's nutrient profile, but its best use is as a spread on top of the garden bed to create a barrier and prevent soil erosion.

Seattle gardeners love this stuff because it is full of beneficial microorganisms and nutrients that make for good soil. Good soil implies better growth and fewer weeds, and that means less work for the gardener. Additionally, Zoo Doo enables you to use water more judiciously and eliminate the use of pesticides, making it an ideal option for sustainable gardening.

For composting tips and information, call the Poop Line at 206-625-POOP.

Non-primate herbivores contribute to Zoo Doo production.

GREEN THUMB

WHAT: Non-profit public zoo

WHERE: Woodland Park Zoo: west entrance at 5500 Phinney Ave. N., east entrance at 750 N. 50th St.

COST: $25 for a two-gallon container, $6.95 for a pint container, $10 for a pint of Worm Doo. Highly discounted bulk pricing available twice yearly at Fecal Fest.

PRO TIP: Bedspread is used in the Woodland Park Rose Garden.

The twice-yearly Fecal Fest, held spring and fall, has become increasingly popular with serious gardeners—so popular that participation is by lottery only, one entry per person. The lottery is the only opportunity to buy Zoo Doo in bulk. The odds of winning the Fecal Fest lottery hover between 30 and 60 percent.

Bulk Zoo Doo is for outdoor use, as it's a little more smelly, but containerized Doo can be used indoors in potted plants.

In 2015, the worms got in on the conservation action with Worm Doo. It's a rich and fertile soil amendment for seedlings and potted plants and can be used indoors.

TRAILER PARK SHOPPING

Where can you get married in a shipping container?

If you looked up the word "mall" in the dictionary, you would find it defined as a large, usually covered shopping area where traffic is not allowed. The Georgetown Trailer Park Mall admittedly misses the mark on all counts, but that's precisely why it's noteworthy.

The Trailer Park Mall is a charmingly kitschy outdoor shopping area that started in 2010 to provide local artists, vintage peddlers, and other creative individuals a space to conduct their businesses sustainably. It's managed out of eight adorable vintage trailers that date back to the 1950s; the longest is 33 feet, and the shortest is 12 feet.

The shop owners claim to be purveyors of the rare and the sublime. While you never know what you'll find, recent offerings have included everything from vintage clothing, retro tins, and typewriters from the '30s to handmade balms, original artwork, and vinyl records. Vendors are knowledgeable and chatty, happy to answer questions or spin a tale about an item for sale.

GEORGETOWN TRAILER PARK MALL

WHAT: Retail shopping

WHERE: In a parking lot at 5805 Airport Way S.

COST: Free to browse. Wedding ceremonies start at $240.

PRO TIP: Wedding licenses in Washington State require a three-day waiting period and are valid for an additional 60 days.

Proprietors at the Georgetown Trailer Park Mall are part retailers and part artists, and they're happy to chat with you while you're browsing.

Get married in a shipping container.

The liveliest time to visit the Georgetown Trailer Park Mall is during the Second Saturday Art Attack. During this time, neighborhood galleries remain open, a shuttle transports guests around to galleries, and lots of art lovers and shoppers are out on the streets.

In the back corner of the mall is a shipping container that houses a wedding chapel. An adjacent vintage trailer is used as a dressing area. Weddings are by appointment only, no spur-of-the-moment getting hitched here. A license is required.

A METROPOLITAN CITY

What was the first US team to win a Stanley Cup?

Until 1914, hockey's Stanley Cup was solely a Canadian trophy. That's the year the New Westminster Royals moved from British Columbia to Portland, Oregon, and became the Rosebuds. The former Canadian team wasn't going to lose out on a championship opportunity, and after that the Stanley Cup championship was for the best hockey team in the world.

Although the Rosebuds were the first American team to play in the Stanley Cup final, on March 26, 1917, the Seattle Metropolitans were the first US team to win the cup. The win was the first major sports championship for Seattle.

In 1919, the Metropolitans were back in the quest for the cup. Unfortunately, the championship series had to be canceled because of the Spanish influenza epidemic, leaving the series with the Montreal Canadiens tied at 2-2-1. The Metropolitans had one more appearance in the Stanley Cup, losing to the Ottawa Senators in 1920, but never regained their winning momentum.

The Metropolitans played at the Seattle Ice Arena, located at a prime spot at the corner of Fifth Avenue and University Street. It was a modern arena that could hold around 4,000 fans and featured an artificially cooled ice surface, and the team could pack in the fans. Unfortunately, this prime location led to their downfall. The newly constructed Olympic Hotel (now the Fairmont Olympic) needed parking for its guests.

RELEASE THE KRAKEN

WHAT: Sports team

WHERE: Climate Pledge Arena, 305 Harrison St.

COST: Tickets not yet available

PRO TIP: The cancellation of the Metropolitan's Stanley Cup series against the Montreal Canadiens was one of only two times the cup was not awarded. The other time was in 2005 as a result of a labor dispute.

Top: *Climate Pledge Arena on the Seattle Center campus is under construction.* Inset: *Kraken merchandise gets Seattle prepped for the return of NHL hockey.*

The University of Washington owned the arena's lease and bought out the final year. They razed the arena and put up a parking lot.

The Seattle Metropolitans folded in 1924 and, despite their success, became largely forgotten. There is nothing in the city that commemorates the Stanley Cup win, no local honors for the five team members inducted into the Hockey Hall of Fame, and the parking lot is now the 20-story 1200 Fifth, formerly the IBM Building. It's almost as if they never existed.

The NHL is returning to Seattle for the 2021-22 season with the Kraken. The name comes from a giant octopus of Norse myth. The Seattle Kraken didn't forget their successful predecessors and have paid tribute to the Metropolitans in the team logo. The team will hit the ice at the new Climate Pledge Arena on the Seattle Center campus.

Climate Pledge Arena will be powered exclusively by renewable energy, making it the world's first zero-carbon arena.

A GHOST WALKED INTO A BAR

Where is there a haunted pub?

Kells is an Irish restaurant and pub located in Post Alley at Seattle's Pike Place Market. This family-owned bar, founded in 1983, belongs to the McAleese family, who wanted to bring Irish traditions and pub culture to Seattle. While it's not as great as being in Ireland, Kells's menu—especially the whiskey and beer selection—will feel like the next best thing.

Apart from its Irish food, drink, and music, Kells is famous for its ghostly activities. A few spirits seem to have become regulars, perhaps explained by the site's history.

The pub is located in the Butterworth building, earlier the location of Seattle's first mortuary. The mortuary was built in the 1900s and stored the bodies of those who had died from violence and disease. The bodies came in through the front door of what is now Kells, were kept in elevators, and were eventually moved to the third floor. The mortuary stored coffins in what is now Kells's banquet room. It's not surprising that paranormal activity is reported, including broken bar glasses, eccentric figures, whispering and banging noises from upstairs, and a chemical formaldehyde aroma.

KELLS IRISH RESTAURANT AND BAR

WHAT: Restaurant and bar

WHERE: 1916 Post Alley

COST: Entrees start at $13. There is a discounted happy hour menu.

PRO TIP: Try the shepherd's pie made with Kells Irish Stout.

Top: *Follow the Post Alley signs to get to Kells and other shops and bars often overlooked at the Market.* Inset: *Kells Irish Restaurant and Bar in Post Alley.*

Two regular spirits include a young girl with long red hair and a man dressed in a white coat. The girl may have been one of the many children who did not recover from the influenza pandemic in 1918. The man, known as Charlie, often appears on the Guinness mirror and then disappears. Both spirits seem to enjoy the pub and have fun, with no intention of frightening or causing harm.

Kells pub, located in Post Alley, has a ghostly history that goes back to a previous life as the site of a mortuary.

RUBBER CHICKEN

Where can you find an assortment of rubber chickens?

For most people, rubber chickens are a comedy prop, a bit of latex shaped like a plucked fowl. Or maybe it's used to refer to one of those chewy, tasteless banquet meals. However, after visiting Archie McPhee, you'll never think about rubber chickens in the same way again.

Founded in 1983, Archie McPhee is a novelty store that sells crazy gag gifts, costumes, and paraphernalia. If you're looking for a white elephant gift exchange idea, you'll find it here. Need a costume for Halloween? Yep, there's a good selection here. Glow-in-the-dark swizzle sticks, unusually flavored candy, politically incorrect t-shirts? They've got it, right along with an impressive selection of action figures.

It's easy to see the store as a bizarre mish-mash of trinkets and doodads, but it's all very neatly categorized and displayed. Sales staff can find an item or make a recommendation in the blink of an eye, although shoppers will likely take forever to make a selection. It can take a long time to decide between kale-flavored hard candy and pizza candy canes. And while the business was built selling factory rejects and pop culture cast-offs, many items are now exclusively created for Archie McPhee.

At the back of the store, overlooked if you don't get back that far, is the Rubber Chicken Museum, opened in 2018. Claiming to be the only such museum in the world, it's more of a roped-off display of curio cabinets full of rubber chickens in

---

Archie McPhee was a jazz musician from the 1920s and a distant relative of the company founder.

Left: *There's a rubber chicken museum at the back of Archie McPhee.* Right: *Archie McPhee is full of fun images and strange characters.*

ARCHIE MCPHEE

WHAT: Store and museum

WHERE: 1300 N. 45th St.

COST: Free to browse

PRO TIP: The bacon mints are not as awful as they might sound.

unimaginable shapes, sizes, and themes. Learn about the history of rubber chickens and why they are such a staple of comedy, and read a scholarly essay from a rubber chicken expert—yes, there is such a thing.

AROUND THE WORLD

Where did the first round-the-world flight start from?

The World Flight Monument is located at one of the entrances to Magnuson Park. If you remember when the park was a military installation—Sand Point Naval Air Station—it's in front of the guard gate entrance. The monument is also known as the Round-the-World Flight Monument and memorializes the beginning and ending point of the first flight that circumnavigated the world.

Created by sculptor Alonzo Victor Lewis, once known as the Washington State Sculptor Laureate, the piece consists of a pair of bronze bird wings atop a tapering concrete tower. The wings signify the four two-seater Douglas biplanes that took off from the naval air station on April 7, 1924.

The Army mission was for the four planes and eight men to circumnavigate the globe, a 26,345-mile journey, and return to the station. They would be the first to accomplish the feat, but men from five other countries were nipping at their heels, trying to beat them.

Not long into the venture, one of the planes crashed into a mountain in Alaska. Fortunately, the crew survived, and the remaining three planes continued with the challenge. Those three planes crossed the Pacific Ocean to Japan, becoming the first Americans to reach that country by air. While this is a routine trip today, in the 1920s it was a dangerous proposition.

One plane ran into engine trouble in Southeast Asia, but a rescue plan was successful, and the three crews reached Paris on

---

WORLD FLIGHT MONUMENT

WHAT: Art and history

WHERE: 7400 Sand Point Way, NE 74th Street entrance to Magnuson Park

COST: Free

PRO TIP: This was an Army mission. The Air Force wasn't founded for another couple of decades.

The World Flight Monument commemorates one of Seattle's many aviation firsts.

Bastille Day. After working on the planes and resting up, it was time to head home. But the final legs of the journey were not without more problems, and one of the planes had mechanical issues that forced it to land on the North Sea. The remaining two planes continued on, returning to Sand Point Naval Air Station 175 days after they began. The United States won the race to circumnavigate the globe by air.

Seattle made aviation history in the race to circumnavigate the globe.

JUST YOUR SELFIE

Where is the best spot for a selfie?

With the rise of Instagram and other social media platforms over the past decade, every location has become a spot for selfies. Museum pros have needed to cope with clamoring visitors more interested in the perfect shot than in the art, history, and culture on offer. Enter the Seattle Selfie Museum. It's not actually a museum, but a space where visitors can take beautifully staged selfies for social media.

The museum has two floors that house installations where people can snap photos. Some of the more popular displays are the gumball machines, giant chopsticks and sushi, bathtub, and mirror room. Additional props are available in some display areas—pillows, chairs, and lights—all designed to get the creative juices flowing and make getting the shot as easy as possible. If you're running low on creativity or feeling overwhelmed, the staff is available to guide you through the options and offer up suggestions.

SEATTLE SELFIE MUSEUM

WHAT: Photo shoot location

WHERE: 92 Union St.

COST: $29 per person for one hour access to all displays. $34 on weekends.

PRO TIP: The mirror room is the most popular installation, so don't save it till last.

The Seattle Selfie Museum isn't a museum. It's two floors of backdrops for staging the perfect selfie.

Snap a selfie in a tub with bubbles.

Professional camera equipment (DSLRs and tripods) is allowed, and on specified dates you can make a selfie date with your dog. On a typical visit, you might see millennials snapping selfies for the 'gram, a high schooler getting their senior photos, a couple looking for the perfect engagement photo background, families with kids, or a group of friends just being silly.

Entry to the museum is in one-hour increments and includes access to all the installations and props. No food is allowed.

A HISTORIC VIEW (page 144)

BRUCE LEE'S FAVORITE RESTAURANT (page 46)

HIT THE TRAIL (page 116)

THESE BOOTS AREN'T MADE FOR WALKING (page 66)

JUST YOUR SELFIE (page 86)

BIG SHOES TO FILL (page 40)

OVERCOMING A TOXIC PAST (page 114)

GET YOUR EXERCISE (page 54)

RINGY DINGY (page 32)

FINS OF NAVAL HISTORY (page 34)

RUBBER CHICKEN (page 82)

A SOUND GARDEN (page 166)

A GARDENING FAMILY (page 164)

IT'S ELECTRIFYING (page 64)

ME GOTTA GO

What song is sung in the seventh inning stretch at Mariner games?

The song "Louie Louie" was written by Richard Berry, with simple lyrics that tell the story of a Jamaican sailor returning home to see his love. The Pharaohs released it as a B-side ballad in 1957, and as the band toured the West Coast it became a regional favorite. The Pharaohs re-released it as an A-side single, but sales never took off.

Five years later, the Kingsmen, a Portland rock and roll band, cobbled together $50 to record and release their version of "Louie Louie." This version wasn't a ballad. Instead, it was a twanging, rocking, more lively rendition of the song. And this time, it caught on, propelling the song and the Kingsmen to national acclaim.

Unfortunately, it wasn't all smooth sailing to a happy ending. Much of the recording was garbled, and the lyrics hard to understand. Although this was caused by poor microphone placement, it wasn't long before rumors circulated claiming the song contained obscenities. These allegations went far beyond merely raising eyebrows, and, eventually, the FBI launched an investigation to determine whether the lyrics were obscene. The investigation likely helped propel the song into prominence; it climbed to No. 2 on the Billboard singles chart, but the FBI found no evidence of profanity.

In the '80s, somewhat as a publicity stunt, there was a grassroots effort to have "Louie Louie" declared the official

LOUIE LOUIE

WHAT: Song

WHERE: Seventh inning stretch at T-Mobile Park

COST: Tours of T-Mobile Park are $12 for adults, $10 for children

PRO TIP: April 11 (Richard Berry's birthday) is celebrated as International Louie Louie Day.

Top: *An entrance to T-Mobile Park on Edgar Martinez Drive.*
Inset: *Safe at home plate.*

Washington State song. It wasn't successful. "Washington My Home" remains the state song, but the Seattle Mariners adopted the music for their seventh-inning stretch. Immediately following "Take Me Out to the Ballgame," the music segues into a rocking version of "Louie Louie."

After failing to be declared the official state song, "Louie Louie" is still played in the seventh inning stretch at Mariner home games.

IN A PICKLE

Where did pickleball start?

Pickleball is a paddleball sport that incorporates elements of badminton, tennis, and table tennis. The game started on Bainbridge Island during the summer of 1965, when Joel Pritchard's family complained of boredom. He decided to set up a game of badminton but couldn't find a shuttlecock. Since necessity is the mother of invention, he cobbled together a made-up game involving what he had at hand—a net, some paddles, and a plastic ball—and pickleball was born.

Pritchard and friends made the first paddles in a Bainbridge Island basement. They were made of wood and shaped like a large ping-pong paddle. The ball was simple and made of plastic with holes all over it. A net was stretched low across the court, and lines were drawn for in and out. The Pritchards and family friends played pickleball all summer, shared the game with neighbors and more friends, and seven years later the game had grown into a manufacturing and sports business. Pritchard would go on to serve as a US congressman, and the family friends operated the business.

Pickleball can be played by two (singles) or four (doubles) players, on a badminton-sized court (20 by 44 feet), with a modified tennis net, and is played indoors or out. The ball is served underhand from alternating sides of the court, and it must bounce at least once before it can be returned. This continues with the usual volleys over the net.

PICKLEBALL

WHAT: Game

WHERE: In your backyard or at courts around the city

COST: Most courts in the area have no fee. Membership in the Seattle Pickleball Network is $4.99 per year.

PRO TIP: You can fit four pickleball courts on a tennis court.

Minimal equipment is required for a game of pickleball.

The winner is the first to reach 11 points, winning by at least two points. Game terminology is similar to other net games: baseline, foot fault, lob, rally, and sideline. If you can follow tennis or badminton, you'll be able to follow pickleball.

The backyard game has grown beyond its roots and is one of the fastest-growing sports in the United States. It can be enjoyed casually by people of all ages and abilities, although a national rating and championship series has evolved. The governing body of the game is USA Pickleball.

Besides backyard play, there are 37 courts in the Seattle area that allow public or school play. Most are outdoors, and there are no court fees. If you want to up your game and become a regular player, you can join the Seattle Pickleball Network.

The game's name comes from Joan Pritchard, who said the game reminded her of the pickle boat in crew where oarsmen were chosen from the leftovers of other boats.

THE ROAR OF THE FALLS

Where is the waterfall featured in the opening credits of *Twin Peaks*?

With over 1.5 million visitors each year, Snoqualmie Falls is one of the most popular scenic attractions in Western Washington (second only to Mount Rainier). Located on the Snoqualmie River, between Snoqualmie and Fall City, the falls are 268 feet high—taller than Niagara Falls. It's less than an hour's drive from downtown Seattle yet feels deep in the heart of nature.

The falls can be viewed from the observation platforms at the top, easily accessible from the parking lot, and a lower platform that involves a short hike. The hike gives you a view of the falls from the side, and along the path is interpretive signage that points out native plants and information. Benches and large logs provide seating spots along the way, so even out-of-shape visitors can make the hike to the bottom. When the rain and snowfall have been extra heavy, the falls look like a sheet of water spanning between the cliffs. At one time, you could hike on the rocks at the bottom of the falls, creeping ridiculously close to the water's edge, but that is no longer permitted.

The falls are famous for their hypnotizing tumble of water but are equally well known for appearing on the mystery-drama television series *Twin Peaks*.

The credits open with a view of Snoqualmie Falls, although a little literary license places it in a more remote location.

SNOQUALMIE FALLS

WHAT: Waterfall

WHERE: 6501 Railroad Ave., Snoqualmie

COST: Free parking in the upper lot, $7 in the lower lot. Rates at Salish Lodge start at around $225 per night.

PRO TIP: The best room at Salish Lodge for a view of the falls is the River View corner room on the fourth floor.

Top: *Snoqualmie Falls from the lower viewing platform.* Inset: *Salish Lodge & Spa overlooks Snoqualmie Falls.*

Salish Lodge & Spa is a luxury resort overlooking the falls. The resort includes a fine dining restaurant, a spa, and spectacular views. To preserve the location's cultural importance and reclaim traditional tribal lands, the Snoqualmie tribe purchased the land around the falls, the resort, the gift shop, and nearby property.

Snoqualmie means moon in the Salish language.

WEDGWOOD ROCKS

What's up with that big rock?

A gigantic rock, rising nearly 20 feet near a Wedgwood neighborhood intersection, is a geological wonder that connects Seattle to the glacial era. Weighing an estimated 1.5 million pounds with a circumference of 80 feet, the Wedgwood rock is tucked away between trees and houses and has no signage. Despite its geological significance, it remains relatively unknown outside of the neighborhood.

The rock was initially known as Lone Rock, later referred to as Big Rock, and then finally dubbed Wedgwood Rock, both for its composition and location. The rock is classified as a glacial erratic, one of six located in the Puget Sound area. A glacial erratic is a formation that is of a size and geological composition inconsistent with rocks known to be indigenous to the site.

How could this happen? The theory is that during the Ice Age some 14,000 years ago, glaciers carried huge rocks and sediments into the Puget Sound region. Extensive research and testing point to the Wedgwood rock originating on Mount Erie, located on Fidalgo Island some 55 miles north of Seattle.

Long before Seattle was a thriving city, American Indians used the rock as a landmark to guide them through the dense forest. It then became part of 160-acre farmland, with ownership of the rock transferring with the property. One property owner authorized the Seattle Mountaineers Club to hone their rock climbing skills on the structure, which was undeveloped at the

THAT'S A BIG ROCK

WHAT: A big rock

WHERE: Intersection of 28th Avenue NE and NE 72nd Street

COST: Free. Unless you're cited for climbing on it

PRO TIP: In 1970, the Seattle City Council instituted a fine of up to $100 for climbing on the rock.

A glacial erratic located in the Wedgwood neighborhood

time. In a subsequent sale, the transfer required the owner to maintain the Wedgwood Rock area as a neighborhood park, but the new owner failed to follow through. A hue and cry from neighborhood citizenry was unsuccessful in persuading the city council to mandate the area be kept as a park.

Today Wedgwood Rock sits by the side of the road, largely ignored. During summer, neighbors and picnickers hang out near the rock, and it serves as a neighborhood meeting spot, but if you are driving by, you likely won't notice it. Don't worry, though; it's not going anywhere.

The topography of the Puget Sound region was caused by a series of Ice Age events.

OVERCOMING A TOXIC PAST

Where was a toxic industrial site turned into a city park?

Gas Works Park was once a Seattle manufacturing hub for synthetic gas production. At the time, synthetic gas was a primary energy source, but the process created significant pollution. The plant pumped out gas and pollution for 50 years during the first half of the 1900s, creating a toxic mess of land and air.

Seattle residents could breathe clean air and a sigh of relief when the plant was officially decommissioned. After decades of abuse, the soil, air, and water had become so devastatingly polluted that the area seemed irreparable. The city bought the property in 1962, kicking off an extensive clean-up plan to turn the site into a public park.

Getting rid of the mess of toxins and pollutants required a multi-part reclamation plan that required community buy-in. The plan called for removing toxins from the land and structures but keeping the facilities and machinery to serve as a reminder of the site's industrial history. Locals embraced the idea of turning the site into a recreational area.

The award-winning project took six years to create a flourishing green space for outdoor recreation. The park includes nearly 20 acres of public area and features a play structure, picnic sites, and paths for cycling, strolling, and jogging. The large structures and machinery that once made up the plant were integrated into the new park and became a part of the city's profile and skyline. They protrude along the shores of Lake Union amidst the lush expanse, providing a curious look back at the city's history.

IT'S NO LONGER A GAS

WHAT: Public park

WHERE: 2101 N. Northlake Way

COST: Free

PRO TIP: Capture a great Seattle skyline photo from an often-overlooked angle.

Remnants of a former gasification plant at Gas Works Park

Gas Works Park was one of the first major industrial site conversions. It serves as an international prototype for creating recreational parks from degraded warehouses, abandoned storage tanks, and industrial spaces and turning eyesores into community gathering places.

The concept of "reduce, reuse, recycle" is exemplified in the blend of industrial and recreational at Gas Works Park.

HIT THE TRAIL

Where is the longest walking trail in Seattle?

Burke-Gilman is a pioneer rail-trail built in the 1970s. A rail-trail is created by converting an old railway track into a multi-use path for public use. Burke-Gilman is a 27-mile paved trail exclusively for non-motorized traffic with multiple points to stop and start. The paved trail is nine feet wide, allowing walkers and cyclists to co-exist while offering some of the best views of Seattle and the surrounding communities.

The trail's starting and ending points are Golden Gardens Park in Ballard and Blyth Park in Bothell. In between, it meanders along the ship canal, Lake Union, and the University of Washington, then heads north through neighborhoods until reaching Magnuson Park on Lake Washington. Passing through still more neighborhoods, it eventually parallels the north edge of Lake Washington before connecting to the Sammamish River Trail in Bothell. The trail goes through energetic urban areas and peaceful parks and along scenic waterways, and it offers some of the best views in Seattle.

BURKE-GILMAN TRAIL

WHAT: Rail trail

WHERE: 27 miles between Ballard and Bothell

COST: Free

PRO TIP: Burke-Gilman Brewing Company is located on the trail and makes a good stopping point.

You can sample Burke-Gilman in bits via numerous access points along the way. Look for opportunities to join the trail in Fremont, Wallingford, the University District, Sand Point, Lake City, Lake Forest Park, or Kenmore. If you're feeling ambitious enough, you can tackle it in one go, taking advantage of neighborhood stops for food and drink, sightseeing, or a short rest.

A segment of the Burke-Gilman Trail running through Sand Point

Burke-Gilman does have a controversial missing link. A section passes through downtown Ballard (on city sidewalks) before rejoining the established trail. This results in breaking the trail up into two sections, short and long. Proposals to close the gap with a mile-and-a-half link remain mired in legal battles, and the connection remains missing.

The Burke-Gilman Trail was named for two Seattle lawyers, Thomas Burke and Daniel Gilman.

SILENCE IN THE CITY

Where can you find a waterfall in downtown Seattle?

In the middle of the crowded city, this Zen-like urban park provides a respite in a heavily trafficked area. It's a peaceful creation of concrete, wood, and water with a waterfall that drowns out nearly all Pioneer Square noise. Take a book, read the paper, or sit and meditate. The Waterfall Garden Park spirit is as calming as the rushing water and makes for a great break from a busy work or touring day.

The 60-by-80-foot pocket park, designed by landscape architect Masao Kinoshita, is open during the day to the public and is closed at night. A 22-foot man-made waterfall is the centerpiece of the park. Five thousand gallons of water are pumped through the waterfall every minute, blocking out traffic noise and providing a white noise background for visitors. Around the waterfall is a Japanese garden with indigenous plants.

There are plenty of tables, chairs, and benches here, and since so many people overlook it, it rarely feels overcrowded. Nearby workers bring their lunch, coffee, or a book to get away from the daily grind. Visitors to the city can often be spotted resting up or reading their guidebook.

The multinational shipping giant UPS has deep roots in Waterfall Garden Park. Originally known as the American Messenger Company, the company began its operations at this

WATERFALL GARDEN PARK

WHAT: Urban park

WHERE: 219 Second Ave. S. (Second and Main)

COST: Free

PRO TIP: If your Zen-like spirit needs to connect to the outside world, you'll find power outlets located throughout.

The often-overlooked Waterfall Garden Park features a 22-foot waterfall at its center.

location in 1907. The company later changed its name to UPS and opened branches across the country.

In 1975, UPS vacated its original premises and set up its headquarters in Connecticut. Waterfall Garden Park was created on the footprint of the business. Today it is maintained by the Annie E. Casey Foundation, named for UPS founder James E. Casey's mother.

Waterfall Garden Park is a pocket park located on the original UPS headquarters' site (then called American Messenger Company).

LET THERE BE LIGHT

Why are so many of Seattle's cocktail lounges dark and gloomy?

Washington State kept blue laws on the books for decades after Prohibition was a distant memory. The prohibition against selling spirits on Sunday wasn't repealed until 2005, and it was another six years before liquor sales at grocery stores were permitted.

Looking back, it seems inconceivable that it wasn't until 1976 that the first daylight bar opened in Seattle. Before that time, the state legislature preferred that citizens enjoy their booze at night—or, at a minimum, kept day-drinking out of sight by hiding bars behind walls and dark windows. Those archaic liquor laws effectively turned cocktail space into dark and gloomy rooms.

Oliver's Lounge was Seattle's first daylight bar, coming about because of two significant changes: the repeal of some of the blue laws and extensive renovations at the Mayflower Park Hotel.

The Mayflower Park Hotel dates back to 1927 and is the oldest continually operating hotel in Seattle. The renovations in the 1970s were to save the hotel from bankruptcy and ultimately make it over with its early history and architecture in mind. The dark hotel bar moved into a corner location with floor-to-ceiling 25-paned windows, repurposed tabletops from a razed local building, and a massive Philippine mahogany bar. The Seattle cocktail scene changed forever.

Old-school bars and cocktail lounges had small windows along the top of the wall as a way to let some light into the room while making sure that no one saw drinkers inside the establishment.

Located on the corner of Fourth and Olive, Oliver's was Seattle's first daylight bar.

The result was a 1,400-square-foot lounge flooded with natural light and a cheery ambiance, even on a gray Seattle day. It maintains its retro-swank atmosphere, a commemorative nod to the hotel's history and Prohibition. Sitting at Oliver's, enjoying one of their signature martinis, it's hard to imagine a time when outdoor and patio cocktails were illegal in Seattle.

FIRST SEATTLE DAYLIGHT BAR

WHAT: Cocktail lounge

WHERE: Fourth and Olive Way, attached to the Mayflower Park Hotel

COST: Martinis and signature cocktails start at $13. Food items start at $6.

PRO TIP: This is a popular spot for professionals enjoying happy hour but is quieter and more romantic in the evening.

121

PLAY A MEAN PINBALL

Where can vintage pinball machines be found?

When you think about pinball, what probably comes to mind is the digital game on your first PC from the '90s, or perhaps the odd, stand-alone hunk of metal gathering dust at your local bowling alley. Charlie Martin, a self-proclaimed "pinhead" and owner of the Seattle Pinball Museum, finds this horrific, which is why he and his wife have made it their mission to preserve and revive pinball for future generations.

He and his wife were bitten by the pinball bug in the mid-2000s and began collecting and restoring the machines at their home. When they ran out of space, they decided to share their collection with the community and moved it into the museum's present location. Although their business is called a museum, it's anything but a traditional museum. Most visitors say it's more like an arcade with its bustling environment and an assortment of free-play games.

Martin says that pinball machines are interactive, kinetic works of art, crediting the collaborative genius of electrical and mechanical engineers, designers, and metal workers. Pinball enthusiasts agree that there's something exhilarating about feeling the ball hit the glass and hearing the flippers flapping away, all in search of that elusive high score.

Amid the wonderland of lights and sounds, the pinball machines are placed in chronological order, enabling you to take

PINBALL MUSEUM

WHAT: Interactive museum and arcade

WHERE: 508 Maynard Ave. S.

COST: $18 adults, $15 kids for a single entry. Admission lets you play all the games.

PRO TIP: If you want to play the machines in chronological order, the best opportunity is during non-peak times such as weekday mornings.

The pinball machines at the Seattle Pinball Museum provide a look at pop culture over the decades.

a trip down pinball memory lane. Each device has fact sheets on it, so you can learn more about the machines you play. There are always at least 50 pinball machines on display at the small storefront. Martin owns many more devices than the space can hold, so he continually circulates the machines in and out to provide a balance of vintage and current machines.

The museum has both vintage and modern models, including games produced by classic manufacturers. If you find yourself hooked playing the silver ball, Martin can provide collecting and purchasing information.

Nudging, a movement of bumping the pinball machine, can make the ball bounce harder from the flipper. Done poorly, however, it can tilt the device.

THE BUILDING THAT LIVES

Where is the greenest building in Seattle?

Feeling fully alive means finding harmony between ourselves and nature. It's difficult enough for people to find and live in harmony, so it might seem impossible to believe that a building could find harmony. Indeed it can, though, as the Bullitt Center proves.

Built to be the greenest commercial building in the world, the Bullitt Center was constructed of materials that are not toxic to people or the environment. It harnesses solar energy and rainwater to meet nearly all of its office needs and consumes 82 percent less energy than an average commercial building. It is certified as a "living building," built in compliance with the International Living Future Institute's uber-stringent environmental standards. The energy efficiency comes in large part from its strange-looking, oversized roof. The center uses 575 rooftop solar panels. The panels generate more electricity than the building uses, creating a surplus that is returned to the grid. It is one of the world's largest "net positive" energy buildings.

Seattle is known for its rain, and that abundant rainwater is harvested and filtered on the roof, then funneled into the building. It meets almost all the water needs of the building, in conjunction with slow-flushing toilets that use foam instead of water to transfer waste into composters kept in the basement. Every practice and policy focuses on well-thought-out consumption habits.

Still, there are some days when cooling is needed. At the Bullitt Center, air conditioning isn't required because the building cools itself through natural ventilation. It has motorized windows that open and close automatically based on the temperature difference between the inside and outside of the building.

Seattle philanthropist Dorothy Bullitt founded the Bullitt Foundation in 1952.

Unusual architectural features help make the Bullitt Center the greenest building in Seattle.

BULLITT CENTER

WHAT: Commercial office building

WHERE: 1501 E. Madison St.

COST: Free

PRO TIP: Tenants at the Bullitt Center are required to commit to energy and water budgets as part of their lease agreements.

All of these features might feel a little risky, but going all-in on a concept is not unusual for Dorothy Bullitt. Known for her tenacious can-do attitude, Bullitt was a Seattle radio and television pioneer. As a young widow, she rebuilt her family's real estate wealth lost during the Depression. She was the first woman in the United States to purchase and manage a television station, building Seattle's successful King Broadcasting Company.

Bullitt was an ardent philanthropist who believed in the importance of her community. She founded the Bullitt Foundation with the mission to protect the Pacific Northwest's natural environment. While she didn't live to see the Bullitt Center completed, there's no doubt that it is consistent with the vision she had for Seattle's future. Fortunately, her children and grandchildren have continued her legacy.

SINKS FULL OF HOPE

What are those sinks all over the University District?

Homelessness is a complex topic to discuss, let alone solve. It's an issue in cities across the United States and is often discussed behind closed doors and away from the general public. Seattle is no different. But groups around Seattle are trying to create community initiatives designed to address this real-world challenge, getting it out into the open and getting it solved.

The Seattle Street Sink Project, initiated by Real Change, is a do-it-yourself solution to install sinks in public places around the city. A safe and clean water supply is an often-overlooked need of the homeless or home-insecure population, especially when public restrooms are not readily available. We all need to be mindful of regular handwashing, and these urban street sinks meet the need for everyday hygiene conveniently and in a way that also preserves dignity. The first street sink was set up near the ROOTS Young Adult Shelter in the University District, and a few more quickly popped up around the neighborhood.

THE SINK PROJECT

WHAT: Community initiative

WHERE: Multiple locations around Seattle

COST: Free

PRO TIP: The sinks are deep enough to allow for washing clothing and other personal belongings.

The sinks can be installed using readily available parts with only basic tools and skills. Generally hosted by nonprofit organizations, the sinks are connected to an outdoor faucet, spigot, garden hose, or other water hookup, providing continual water access. They never require refilling, and the used water drains into a connected trough filled with plants and flowers, creating neighborhood beautification.

Located around the city, Seattle Street Sinks provide water to people in need.

With some public funding recently secured, around 60 more street sinks will be set up at strategic spots around Seattle. The sinks can be spotted by the bright blue sticker on the side.

The Clean Hands Collective, a collaborative community organization that promotes hand hygiene, developed the Seattle Street Sink design.

THE ROAR OF THUNDER BOATS

Where can vintage hydroplanes and racing memorabilia be found?

Every August since 1951, Lake Washington and the Seafair Cup race have been the center of the universe for hydroplane racing. The annual race brings together H1 Unlimited hydroplane drivers from across the country to compete for the coveted Seafair Cup. Starting with the qualifying time trials right on through to the flag drop for the "winner take all" final heat, it's an exciting weekend of hydroplane racing.

If seeing the boats once a year isn't satisfying enough, the Hydroplane and Raceboat Museum in Kent will feed your love for hydroplane racing all year long. The museum is like a time capsule that takes you back to the early days of racing, with dozens of vintage hydroplanes on display, many of them still operational.

The exhibits enable you to get up close and personal with your favorite hydroplanes. Long-time fans will get excited over classics such as the *Miss Bardahl*, *Oh Boy! Oberto*, and the *Slo-mo-shun V*, boats that baby boomer fans will remember racing live on Lake Washington. If you ever wanted a chance to see the cockpits, controls, and engines, this is it. No climbing aboard, however.

Visitors to the museum are there to do more than just see the hydroplanes, though. It's more of an interactive trip down memory lane, a chance to relive and talk about the excitement of past races. Memorabilia on display, including helmets, time clocks, patches, and trophies, are sure to get the conversations going.

The Seafair hydro races are the longest continuously running event on the racing schedule.

The Miss Budweiser *is one of the classic hydroplanes on display at the Hydroplane and Raceboat Museum.*

Hydroplane racing has its sobering reminders that racing on the water at nearly 200 miles per hour is inherently dangerous. The sport has had its share of fatalities, including legendary driver Bill Muncey, who died in a spectacular blow over crash. He has long been considered the top hydroplane driver of all time, and his performances on Lake Washington made him a Seattle fan favorite.

Local racing teams and drivers get their share of recognition, including Seattle driver Chip Hanauer, who piloted the *Squire Shop*, *Atlas Van Lines*, and the *Miss Budweiser*, and Port Orchard driver Dave Villwock, who later drove the *Miss Budweiser*.

HYDROPLANE AND RACEBOAT MUSEUM

WHAT: Sports museum

WHERE: 5917 S. 196th St., Kent

COST: $10 general admission, $5 seniors and students

PRO TIP: During Seafair, vintage hydroplanes take a few laps around the course. Many of the boats are driven by museum volunteers.

A TRIBUTE TO FISHERMEN

Where are all the fishermen?

Hundreds of fishing boats are docked at Fishermen's Terminal in Ballard, fully functional boats that spend months on end fishing off Alaska's coast. There's the random pleasure boat in the mix, but priority is given to commercial craft.

Commercial fishing can be a hazardous occupation. If you've watched *Deadliest Catch* (some of their boats are based here), you'll know what I mean.

Rising above Fishermen's Terminal, between docks eight and nine, is a towering 30-foot monument that pays tribute to the lives of fishers lost at sea. Dedicated in 1988, it features a stone column of an adult male clutching a fishing line with a fish affixed at the end of the line. On both sides of the sculpture, creating a small plaza, are bronze plaques listing the names of over 670 fishermen who've died at sea. Names are added to the plaque every May in an annual memorial ceremony.

But the monument does more than pay tribute to the lives of men and women who perished while engaged in commercial fishing. It offers a special place for closure, reflection, and healing for many families in the fishing community. The annual memorial ceremony and sculpture provide mourners with a chance to pay last respects to loved ones, including all too many who disappeared into the sea and were never recovered.

Over 40 percent of the United States' seafood passes through Seattle on its way south from Alaska—halibut, salmon, crab, and more. A seafood store operates in the central area of the terminal.

FISHERMEN'S MEMORIAL

WHAT: Memorial and market

WHERE: 3919 18th Ave. W.

COST: Free

PRO TIP: Wear flat, non-slip shoes and bring cash to buy the freshest seafood right off the docks.

The Fishermen's Memorial is set against a backdrop of commercial fishing vessels.

Service staff will help you select your seafood, offer up cooking and preparation recommendations, and answer questions. There are no frills and the floor is wet, but there's no denying the seafood's tasty freshness.

For great pricing, head to the docks, cut out the middleman, and buy direct from the fishermen. There will be signage posted as you enter the parking lot of the terminal referencing what seafood is available that day and the dock to buy it.

Every March, to mark the start of the fishing season, a Blessing of the Fleet is held asking God's blessing for a bountiful season, peace upon the unpredictable sea, and a safe journey home.

WALKING ON GLASS

Where can you find glass sidewalks?

When Pioneer Square was first settled, the neighborhood and its streets were much lower than they are today. Too low, in fact, as flooding and sewage overflow into the streets were common occurrences when the tide changed.

After the devastation from the Great Seattle Fire in 1889, the neighborhood was rebuilt higher than before. The ambitious reconstruction tackled the rebuilding after the fire and also took on the city's drainage and sewage problems. The plan called for the city to be rebuilt the equivalent of one floor higher than it was initially, and as a result a substantial underground remained.

The underground's ceiling did double duty as a part of the new sidewalks. Clear glass prisms were built into the new sidewalks to allow natural lighting to stream into the otherwise dark and dingy passageways below.

Over the years, the clear glass prisms aged and changed colors because of exposure to the sun and elements. Some took on a yellow hue, but most have aged into a grayish-purple color. If you aren't looking down while you're walking, you may not even notice them because they blend in with the sidewalk. The prisms were replaced when they became damaged long after light was needed for the underground. Originally, replacements were made from standardized clear prisms, but as aging took its toll and turned the sidewalk-ceiling into a mish-mash of color, the replacements were dyed to match the aged glass. You'll now find fairly consistent coloring in the sidewalks around Pioneer Square.

The original Seattle sidewalks became underground storage, tunnels, and workspaces after the Great Seattle Fire. They were a handy place to hide liquor during Prohibition.

The glass prisms in Pioneer Square's sidewalks were originally designed to light the subterranean passageways created in the aftermath of the Great Seattle Fire.

Replacing the prisms, however, is not an easy or inexpensive choice. Much of the area where repairs are needed is privately owned, and repairs are the property owners' responsibility. Many of these owners are not financially situated to replace the worn-out glass. Various neighborhood stakeholders have collaborated for funding campaigns to cover the cost of replacing the glass, and have also created comprehensive guides on how to embed and maintain them. For now, the glass in the sidewalks remains.

GLASS PRISMS IN THE SIDEWALK

WHAT: Remnants of Seattle after the Great Fire

WHERE: Pioneer Square neighborhood

COST: Free

PRO TIP: On a Seattle Underground Tour, you'll see the glass sidewalks as glass ceilings. The glass doesn't let in as much light as it used to.

FRANKLIN DELANO ROOSEVELT'S TRAIN

Where can you dine amidst presidential history?

The Orient Express is known for its Asian food, karaoke music, and stiff drinks. But there's some fascinating history behind this collection of seven brightly painted and repurposed train cars that have been converted into a restaurant.

The restaurant-in-a-train-car idea started as Andy's Diner, founded by an uncle/nephew duo of Andys—Andy Nagy and Andy Yurkanin. They began with a single railcar. The train car restaurant was a great hit, especially with lunchtime customers from the industrial areas south of the central business district. It was not unusual for the restaurant to serve more than 1,000 people during lunchtime.

More train cars were added, coming from Seattle City Light's Skagit dam construction project and from a Seattle salvage yard. The most valuable acquisition was the train car that Franklin and Eleanor Roosevelt rode during the presidential re-election campaign in 1944. The Andys purchased the car for a cool $18,000 in the 1980s. Not a bad price for a piece of presidential history.

PRESIDENT ROOSEVELT'S TRAIN CAR

WHAT: Restaurant

WHERE: 2963 Fourth Ave. S.

COST: Entrees start at around $12.

PRO TIP: It's said that at least one of the train cars is haunted.

Despite some naysayers claiming that Franklin and Eleanor Roosevelt never rode in this train car, there is sufficient evidence to support the claim.

This bright yellow train car was once Andy's Diner, and before that it was a part of FDR's reelection campaign.

The car is painted bright yellow, with an imposing interior fitted with hardwood panels reminiscent of presidential glory. Photos of President Roosevelt dot the cabin's interior, adding to the theme. An exterior plaque and seal complete the memorialization.

Reservations are required for presidential car dining, and it's generally booked for groups and special events. Visitors can occasionally get a quick peek if the car isn't in use. A polite request to your server will often do the trick. Alternatively, you can try to get a glimpse from the street looking in—you'll probably need to stand on tip-toes to get a good look.

The pair of Andys ran the restaurant business until 1991, adding train cars until they numbered seven. When retirement and death struck, the restaurant changed hands a couple of times before emerging as the Orient Express.

The seven train cars are still there, including the presidential car. It's looking a little shabby around the edges, though, but then FDR wasn't eating Chinese food and singing karaoke.

A SUPER SALESMAN

How did Tacoma become the City of Destiny?

In front of the Wheelock Library in Tacoma's Proctor neighborhood stands a bronze statue of Allen C. Mason, an obscure but influential figure in Tacoma's history. The bronze sculpture depicts Mason with a welcoming, outstretched hand.

Arriving in Tacoma in 1883, Mason became a millionaire best known for passionately selling Tacoma and attracting investment and real estate buyers. He was born in Chicago, Illinois, in 1855 and was entrepreneurial from an early age. He attended college to become a teacher and later studied the law. When he arrived in Tacoma, he had $2.85 in his pocket, and with that he opened a law practice to make a living.

Mason ventured into real estate and prospered, becoming Tacoma's first millionaire. He bought low-cost land north of the city, now the Proctor District, then subdivided it into lots for individual homes. To support this urban expansion, he was instrumental in getting bridges and streetcar lines established, both to make the locations desirable to live in and as a way to increase property values.

To further make the neighborhood desirable, Mason donated land to the city of Tacoma for a park. While land was being cleared to create the park, now known as Puget Park, gold was found on the site. It was the real thing, but there wasn't a sufficient amount of gold found to result in any real value.

Mason aggressively advertised Tacoma as the perfect investment and residential destination in papers all across the

Tacoma is known as the "City of Destiny" due to an advertising campaign to promote the city's livability.

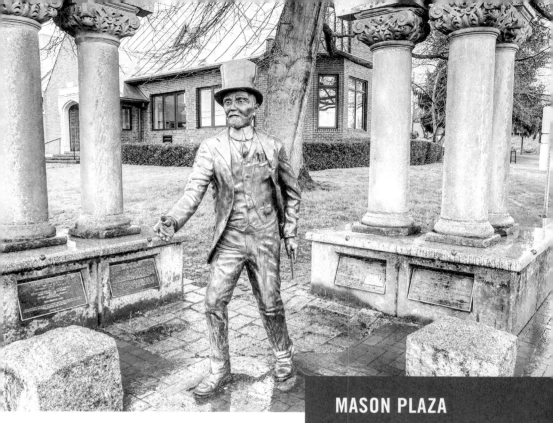

Allen C. Mason welcomes you to Tacoma.

MASON PLAZA

WHAT: Library plaza

WHERE: 3722 N. 26th St., Tacoma

COST: Free

PRO TIP: It is believed that shaking the statue's hand will bring good luck.

country. He coined the term "City of Destiny," and one of his most popular advertisements featured 100 selling points about living in Tacoma. By all accounts, and unlike many developers of this century, Mason was an industrialist with a heart. During the Panic of 1893, he bought back homes from those who were unable to pay for them at fair market value, losing his fortune by doing so. He was only 37 years old.

The legacy of Mason lives on, not only in the plaza and statuary that bear his name but also in how his love for Tacoma shaped its development.

IT FLOATS

Where can you find the longest floating bridge in the world?

At 7,710 feet, the Evergreen Point Floating Bridge, also known as the 520 Bridge, is the world's longest floating bridge. It connects Seattle with the eastside suburban communities of Bellevue, Redmond, and Kirkland, with endpoints in Montlake (near the University of Washington) and Medina. The bridge is officially named the Governor Albert D. Rosellini Bridge. No one calls it that.

The bridge was built to replace the previous floating bridge, which had also been the longest floating bridge in the world. The former bridge had a good run of service but had outlived its design life. New technology for wind and earthquake survivability was needed along with other safety improvements, so a new bridge was constructed.

The new bridge opened in 2016, built a few feet away from the previous bridge, and with an additional 130 feet of length set a new world record. It features an elevated road that enables traffic to avoid waves splashing up, over, and onto the highway—a significant safety improvement. The new bridge has six vehicle lanes, a bicycle path, and a pedestrian path.

Washington State is home to four of the world's five longest floating bridges. At #2 is the Lacey V. Murrow Memorial Bridge (eastbound lanes of I-90 between Seattle and Mercer Island); at #3 is the Hood Canal Bridge (SR 104 connecting the Olympic and

EVERGREEN POINT FLOATING BRIDGE

WHAT: Floating bridge

WHERE: Crossing Lake Washington between Montlake and Medina

COST: $1.25-$2.65, varying based on time of day. Tolls are collected in both directions.

PRO TIP: An average of 74,000 vehicles per day cross the floating bridge.

The Evergreen Point Floating Bridge connects Seattle and the Eastside.

Kitsap peninsulas); and at #5 is the Homer M. Hadley Memorial Bridge (westbound and reversible lanes of I-90 between Mercer Island and Seattle).

Why are floating bridges so popular in Seattle? Like many things in urban planning, it comes down to money.

Lake Washington is a deep lake, over 200 feet in some spots, with soil on the bottom made up of volcanic ash sediment. That composition is very soft, making it costly to do the drilling and excavation for a traditional bridge. A suspension bridge would require towers nearly as tall as the Space Needle, which would be too expensive.

The concept of a floating bridge over Lake Washington came from Seattle engineer Homer M. Hadley. He started with the idea that concrete pontoons had been successfully used for barge-building during World War I. From there, the project grew into the modern-day floating bridge.

The Evergreen Point Floating Bridge holds the Guinness World Records as both the longest and broadest floating bridge.

A JOURNEY COMPLETED

What is the significance of dolphins at the airport?

Dolphins are an integral part of a Native American myth. The goddess Hutash created a Rainbow Bridge to ferry the Chumash people from their congested island to the mainland. Hutash warned her people against looking down into the water during the crossing. Those who failed to heed her warning fell into the waters and would have drowned were it not for her intervention. Hutash rescued lost souls from death by turning them into dolphins. They survived, albeit in another form.

On January 31, 2000, Alaska Airlines Flight 261 was scheduled to fly from Puerto Vallarta, Mexico, to Seattle, with an intermediate stop in San Francisco. As the flight entered airspace over Southern California, critical mechanical problems occurred. Realizing that the problems were insurmountable, the pilots flew the plane away from land and out over the water. Flight 261 crashed into the Pacific Ocean in the Channel Islands near Port Hueneme. All 83 passengers, along with the three flight attendants and two pilots, perished.

As search and rescue efforts began, later turning to search and recover, pods of dolphins were spotted circling the area. As the Chumash legend became more widely circulated among those at the crash site, the dolphins' appearance took on a more profound, spiritual meaning. When a memorial was erected near Port Hueneme, no one was surprised that dolphins were featured prominently in the work of sculptor

---

Alaska Airlines is headquartered in and has its primary operations hub in Seattle. It is the fifth-largest airline in the United States.

Bronze dolphin benches at Sea-Tac Airport pay tribute to Alaska Airlines Flight 261.

DOLPHINS RETURNING HOME

WHAT: Bronze dolphin benches

WHERE: Third floor of the parking garage at the north end of Sea-Tac Airport

COST: Free

PRO TIP: Sculptor Bud Bottoms also designed a dancing dolphin fountain that's in Puerto Vallarta, the origination city of Flight 261.

Bud Bottoms—a large bronze sundial and three dolphins.

Nearly 21 years after the loss of Flight #261, the dolphins arrived in Seattle. Located in the Ground Transportation Plaza at Sea-Tac Airport, two bronze dolphin benches memorialize the lives lost. Bottoms had passed away, but his molds were used to cast the benches, instilling a theme of continuity and community. Although the dolphins were designed for children to sit and play on and their significance may be lost over time, they remain a symbol of a journey finally completed.

MUSICAL SLUMBER PARTY

Does Seattle have a waterfront hotel?

The Edgewater Hotel is a four-story waterfront property built on a pier over Elliott Bay. It was initially built for the Seattle World's Fair, providing an impressive waterfront location for visitors to the city. Construction restrictions no longer allow for pier construction, so the Edgewater remains Seattle's only waterfront hotel.

The Beatles stayed at the Edgewater in 1964 while on tour, during the height of Beatlemania. Security was so tight, and fans were so determined to see them, that the band had to be transported to the hotel via ambulance. It didn't completely keep fans in the dark as to their whereabouts, but it helped. The hotel had to put up barriers around the property and even keep an eye out for crazed fans swimming across Elliott Bay to catch a glimpse of the band. The Fab Four's stay at the Edgewater has been memorialized in a famous photo showing the mop-tops fishing off the balcony into Elliott Bay.

The fame and popularity of the Beatles rubbed off onto the Edgewater. Everyone wanted to stay where the Beatles stayed, fish where the Beatles fished, and capture a bit of second-hand fame.

Other musicians have stayed at the Edgewater, giving it a continuing music connection. Led Zeppelin stayed at the hotel, with antics that no one wants to confirm or deny, other than to say that the band has been banned from any future stay. Frank Zappa (allegedly) caught a mudshark off the balcony and kept it alive in the bathtub. Guests could purchase bait in the hotel gift shop.

Although they may be the most fun to talk about, it's not just the badly behaved who give the Edgewater its musical street cred.

MUSICAL SUITES

WHAT: Hotel

WHERE: 2411 Alaskan Way

COST: Room rates start at around $300/night, with the music suites starting at around $1,050.

PRO TIP: Don't try to fish off the balcony. It's no longer permitted.

Eddie Vedder of Pearl Jam was involved with the whale mural, which celebrates Seattle's orca J pod. A long list of legendary artists, spanning genres and generations, have called the Edgewater home while performing in Seattle.

To capitalize on this music cachet, the Edgewater has two music-themed suites honoring the Beatles and Pearl Jam. Both suites are filled with special touches and memorabilia that give a nod to these two legendary bands' careers.

Jam out on a guitar, listen to music, or live like a rock star. Even if only for one night.

The Edgewater Hotel holds bragging rights as Seattle's only hotel built directly on the water.

A HISTORIC VIEW

Where was the first skyscraper in Seattle?

For over 50 years, the 38-story, neoclassical Smith Tower was the tallest building in Seattle's skyline. For over a decade, it was the tallest building west of the Mississippi, and for nearly half a century, it was the tallest building on the West Coast. The Space Needle set a new record in 1962. Fast forward to today, and Seattle has over a dozen skyscrapers, including the Columbia Center, which is more than twice the height of the Smith Tower.

Named after its builder, L. C. Smith, one of the Smith Corona typewriter company founders, the building was initially planned to be much smaller. Smith's son convinced him to think big—or at least tall enough to grab bragging rights from the National Realty Building (now KeyBank Center) in neighboring Tacoma.

On opening day, 4,200 people rode the brass elevators to the 35th-floor observation deck, paying 25 cents for the ride. The elevators were ornate and sophisticated, with latticed scissor gates over glass doors that gave riders a peek at each floor they passed. Elevator operators staffed the Smith Tower until 2017, when the system was automated and modernized, although one operator remains as a tour guide. The elegant look remains, and there are still glass doors that let riders look into hallways and lobbies.

The observation deck on the 35th floor is one of the best spots for views of the Seattle area. You can see the Olympic and Cascade mountain ranges, Mount Rainier, and Puget Sound on a clear day. Views in Seattle are always dependent on the weather.

The Smith Tower's outer skin is granite on the first two floors, and on the remaining floors is terra cotta. The exterior of the building has been washed only once, in 1976.

WHAT: Historic building

WHERE: 506 Second Ave.

COST: $29 for tower tours, $16 access for observation deck and bar (discount for Washington State residents)

PRO TIP: If you plan to be a regular, the Rum-Runner's Card gives you year-long access to Smith Tower, including additional food and beverage discounts and guest privileges, for $99.

With its neoclassical architecture and pyramid top, it's easy to spot the Smith Tower in the Seattle skyline.

The interior of the 35th floor is the Prohibition-themed Observatory Bar. A popular spot next to the bar is the Wishing Chair. Rumors about the chair abound, including about its origin. One story claims the chair was a gift from China's Empress Dowager Cixi back in 1908. Another persistent legend holds that an unmarried person who sits in the chair will be married within a year.

The Smith Tower is home to business and professional offices, special events space, historical exhibits, and a ground floor gift shop in addition to the observation deck.

A pyramid-shaped penthouse is on the top floors of the building. For the first time since a building renovation created the apartment in the late 1990s, it is available for lease. The 2,128-square-foot apartment is on two levels, with a catwalk surrounding the living room, and offers sweeping views of the city through its triangle-shaped windows. The listing price is $17,000 per month on a long-term lease.

KEEP CLAM

Who was the Mayor of the Waterfront?

Ivar Haglund was born in Seattle, the son of Scandinavian immigrants. He lived a full life, clocking in nearly eight decades, and was a folk singer, bohemian, restaurateur, and port commissioner. Haglund was a master of self-promotion, often a shameless huckster, which led to his being dubbed the Mayor of the Waterfront. However, of all his traits, the one he is most remembered for is his eternal love for his hometown.

Graduating from the University of Washington with a degree in economics, Haglund intended to become a stockbroker. The onset of the Great Depression cut short that career path, forcing him into nontraditional work as a folk singer and entertainer. It was the beginning of what would become a life of serial entrepreneurship.

Haglund's first entrepreneurial endeavor was starting Seattle's first aquarium in 1938. From a location on Pier 54, he convinced curious visitors to part with a nickel for a look at the fascinating marine life from Puget Sound. Since aquarium visitors would get hungry, Haglund started selling fish and chips. Before long, his clientele went far beyond the aquarium patrons, and the little fish-and-chip shack grew into Ivar's Acres of Clams.

When it came to marketing hijinks, Haglund had no shame. He sponsored clam eating contests and octopus wrestling contests and created giant clams that made appearances at local events. He'd stroll the business district with Patsy, his pet seal, and even tried to create a

IVAR'S ACRES OF CLAMS

WHAT: Folk hero and restaurateur

WHERE: 1001 Alaskan Way, and 22 other locations around the greater Seattle area

COST: Varies

PRO TIP: You can still feed the seagulls at Ivar's Acres of Clams as long as it's not in a covered eating area.

Ivar's Acres of Clams has been a waterfront institution for over 80 years.

clam postage stamp. His acumen for publicity stunts grabbed media attention but often put him at odds with his business neighbors and the city council.

When neighboring businesses put up "Please don't feed the seagulls" signs, Haglund posted a sign that said, "Seagulls welcome! Seagull lovers welcome to feed seagulls in need." A variation of this sign is still posted today. Postal inspectors didn't find his faux postage stamps—with a clam on them, of course—amusing at all.

As Haglund's restaurant businesses expanded throughout the greater Seattle area, he remained quick with a pun and a witty reply. He gave back to his beloved community by sponsoring Fourth of July fireworks, cleverly billed as Fourth of Jul-Ivar, for over 40 years.

And at his passing, Haglund left substantial endowments to his alma mater, the University of Washington School of Business, and the restaurant program at Washington State University. The number of Seattle-ites who remember Haglund as more than just a name on a chain of restaurants is dwindling, but his endowments will help keep his entrepreneurial spirit alive for generations to come.

Some of what has been written about Ivar Haglund is more folk legend than truth. That includes here.

GOING BATTY

Where can bats be found?

In 1996, 33 bat lovers formed a group devoted to studying and preserving bats in the Pacific Northwest. Bats Northwest later incorporated, officially creating a nonprofit corporation. Bats Northwest works with other agencies, such as the Washington Department of Natural Resources, the Washington State Department of Fish and Wildlife, and the local park systems, to provide habitat for bats and protect them.

Bats Northwest's mission is to raise awareness about the importance of bats, helping residents understand and appreciate the crucial role bats play in maintaining an ecological balance. To further this goal, the organization partners with biologists and researchers to provide speakers at community events. They also conduct professional workshops where pest control operators, environmentalists, naturalists, and health workers educate the public through presentations and informative talks. The group is not just for experts; members of the general public are welcome to join and attend monthly meetings and other events. When you know more about bats, you're able to distinguish fact from fiction, which is a good thing for the bats, residents, and the environment. A big project for Bats Northwest is developing a bat house program in conjunction with health department officials that enables people and bats to coexist and keep both safe.

Unlike birds, bats need an airtight home placed in full sun. They are messy, so you may want to mount the home on a pole in your

BAT HOUSES

WHAT: Conservation effort

WHERE: Your backyard or neighborhood

COST: A ready-made bat house starts around $25.

PRO TIP: Bats are mammals and have belly buttons. Join a bat walk to learn more unusual facts about bats.

Up to 75 bats can live in this bat house.

yard away from the house. Having the bat house in your yard also makes it easier to watch for them. Fragrant flowers and plants can help attract a bat to a new home, but it can still take up to two years for it to be populated. Once bats find the house, a colony of a hundred or more can occupy a home that's two feet high. Installing a bat home comes with a complete set of pros and cons, and Bats Northwest is eager to provide information to help residents decide what's right for them.

About 15 bat species are found in the Pacific Northwest. Since they are nocturnal, they aren't often seen. They hibernate during the winter and are most active during the spring and summer. And, despite the cliche, bats are not blind—they have excellent eyesight.

Bats feast on mosquitoes and are an environmentally friendly option to get rid of pests and protect forests and crops.

NORTH TO ALASKA

How did Seattle prosper during the Gold Rush?

The summer of 1897 was a turning point in Seattle's history. It might have remained a sleepy little waterfront community had it not been for one thing—gold. That summer, the steamer *Portland* cruised into Puget Sound filled with miners who had struck it rich in the Yukon. As a result, Seattle became the outfitting location for miners heading north, resulting in a doubling of the population.

The Klondike Gold Rush National Historical Park is one of only a few in the National Park Service system that spans multiple locations. One unit of the park is in Seattle, and there are three additional units in Skagway, Alaska. All four units are part of the National Park Service system.

You'd be forgiven if you didn't know this National Park site existed as it is housed in the rather anonymous-looking Cadillac Hotel. The hotel served as an outfitter for departing miners and was one of their last stops for provisions before they headed north to the Yukon.

The park takes visitors through staging areas, starting with planning the trip north and finishing with stories from the goldfields. It was a grueling, hard life and was filled with more disillusionment and shattered dreams than fame and fortune, with most miners returning to Seattle with nothing in their pockets.

Very few people hit it big, and most of those who did were the merchants and suppliers, not those in the goldfields. Merchants created outfits, a package of clothing, food, and equipment that a prospector would need for the trip north. A typical outfit would include clothing and boots, nonperishable foods, basic first

KLONDIKE GOLD RUSH HISTORIC SITE

WHAT: National historical park

WHERE: 319 Second Ave. S.

COST: Free

PRO TIP: Purchase a National Parks Passport ($10) and get it stamped at every national park site you visit.

An outfitting kit for heading north during the Klondike Gold Rush

aid supplies, soap, and tools. The outfit, which averaged $250-500, had to last two people for several months. There were few opportunities to replenish supplies once in the Yukon.

Some of the big gold rush winners became household names in Seattle—merchant John Nordstrom invested in a shoe store that grew into the Nordstrom chain of department stores, and Edward Nordhoff founded what became the local Bon Marche department store.

Seattle was reeling from an economic recession and a devastating fire, and the Yukon Gold Rush provided a lifeline. It became a turning point in the city's economic history.

BUCKET OF BLOOD

Where was Seattle's most famous speakeasy?

In the Roaring Twenties, an economic boom created a period of prosperity characterized by vibrant jazz clubs, decked-out flappers, and bootleggers flouting Prohibition laws. It was undoubtedly a time of affluence and artistic dynamism. Speakeasies were the place to soak it all in, and they flourished in the International District. But as laws changed, the neighborhood and attitudes changed. Buildings that housed speakeasies were lost amid urban development.

In 2018, during a renovation of the Louisa Hotel, life-sized Art Deco murals from the jazz era were discovered. Although the hotel owners knew of the hotel's colorful past, complete with secret escape routes and chutes for bootlegged hooch, the murals, hidden beneath layers of plaster, were a surprise.

The Louisa Hotel was built in 1909 to house Asian migrants before they traveled to Alaska. In later years during Prohibition, it hosted two speakeasies in its basement. On the west side was the Blue Heaven, which the infamous Wah Mee Club later occupied. On the east side was Club Royale, popularly called Bucket of Blood because it served liquor in large pails. The club catered to semi-affluent Chinese businesspeople and hosted prominent jazz musicians. The jazz music was so loud that when the club was raided and shut down in 1931, patrons didn't even hear it happening until officers were on the stage handcuffing the piano player.

BUCKET OF BLOOD

WHAT: Art

WHERE: 669 S. King St.

COST: Free

PRO TIP: Jimi Hendrix's mother, Lucille, was a waitress at the Bucket of Blood and occasionally sang there.

The Louisa Hotel once housed a speakeasy.

The murals were found in a narrow staircase leading down to where the club would have been. They had Art Deco lettering that said "Club Royale." With the women in the paintings dressed in furs and men in tuxedos, the murals offered a glimpse into the past at Seattle's bustling jazz scene. The murals also confirmed that jazz clubs were a place where patrons of different races and cultures integrated. During a period of segregation, music could break color and other social barriers to unite communities.

Historians and preservationists worked to preserve the discovered murals and artifacts. They also restored the building's upper floors for its original purpose of providing housing to low-income families. The Louisa Hotel's racy past lives on as both a historic landmark and a source of affordable community housing.

The Louisa Hotel is located in the Wah Mee building, the site of one of Seattle's deadliest massacres.

KEEP JIVING

Where can you have a drink in a coffee pot-shaped building?

The coffee pot–shaped Java Jive has a colorful, if not always verifiable, history. Budding rock stars played there, and couples danced the night away. It was a live music venue and also hosted novelty entertainment like hobby horse races. During Prohibition, it was a speakeasy and gambling hall, entered through a secret door in the women's restroom. And during its incarnation as a tropical paradise, two macaque monkeys (named Java and Jive) lived in an adjacent space.

Built in 1927 by Tacoma resident Otis G. Button, the business was first called the Coffee Pot Restaurant, a descriptive moniker for a 25-foot-high coffee pot–shaped concrete structure. It took on its current name, Bob's Java Jive, under new ownership in 1955.

Owner Bob Radonich turned Java Jive into a music club featuring local bands. The Ventures served as the house band for a while. They made $40 per night, much less than they would make once going on to national prominence. Bing Crosby would stop by with friends when he was in the area. During their formative years, Nirvana performed at the Java Jive. They lasted 10 minutes on stage before being booted off; Radonich didn't like their music.

Java Jive has seen a lot of life pass through its doors, which helped contribute to the building's addition to the National Register of Historic Places.

BOB'S JAVA JIVE

WHAT: Restaurant and bar

WHERE: 2102 S. Tacoma Way, Tacoma

COST: Varies

PRO TIP: Desi Arnaz Jr. added graffiti to one of the booths, scribbling "Ricky Ricardo drank beer her" [sic].

The kitschy Bob's Java Jive is shaped like a coffee pot.

Danette Staatz, Radonich's daughter, now owns and operates the Java Jive. Being listed on the historic registry protects the coffee pot from demolition, but that protection hasn't translated into commercial success. Since its heyday in the 1960s and '70s, it's struggled to survive.

New features and entertainment have been added. There's still live music, although less frequently, and karaoke has been added. The venue is available for private parties and special event rentals. There's almost always a fundraiser or benefit in the works to save the business. Java Jive may be slowing down, but it's not throwing in the towel—it's the little coffee pot that could.

The coffee pot-shaped tavern was named after the 1940 hit "Java Jive" by the Ink Spots.

NO FALLOUT

Is there a fallout shelter in Seattle?

Beneath the Ravenna Bridge, camouflaged by plants, trees, and a little graffiti, is a locked concrete door. You'll pass right by it if you aren't looking for it. Or maybe you'll spot the No Trespassing sign that the Washington State Department of Transportation posted.

The facility was built as a fallout shelter during the Cold War as part of a federal-state partnership. Initially the plan was to build an extensive network of shelters beneath bridges throughout the United States. Upon closer reflection, however, the plan's futility was apparent, and the Ravenna location is the only shelter of its kind. The shelter is considered part of the bridge because it provides partial support, so the Department of Transportation manages the site.

The shelter is approximately 3,000 square feet and was designed to accommodate 200 people. It had seating, a kitchen where canned food could be distributed (although no cooking facilities), and decontamination showers. It was a self-sufficient unit with a well to provide water, a diesel generator, and radiation protection. It was built for survival, not comfort, and fortunately it never had to be used.

If you're a baby boomer, the location may feel familiar as the place you went to get your driver's license. It became a licensing office when it was clear that it was no longer needed as a shelter. After that, it spent years as a DOT storage unit, largely abandoned and forgotten.

The years of disuse made the facility a target for trespassers, who would cut off the locks to gain entry. DOT opened the site to remove

---

The fallout shelter beneath the Ravenna Bridge was built in 1962 at an approximate cost of $65,000. That would be over $512,000 if calculated to present value.

This fallout shelter was, fortunately, never used.

ABANDONED FALLOUT SHELTER

WHAT: Abandoned bomb shelter from the Cold War

WHERE: Beneath the southbound lanes of I-5 at the north end of the Ravenna Bridge

COST: Free

PRO TIP: If you had needed to shelter from a nuclear attack, you would have been given a can of food for dinner, along with the instructions to warm it in your armpit.

some furniture and other items, and afterward the place was again largely forgotten—until it came time for a bridge inspection. Since the examination had to include the shelter below the bridge, DOT got involved again.

This time, when DOT opened the site, its History and Archaeology Department was involved. They found old metal folding chairs and a rotary dial phone. There was a calendar planner and odds and ends of office remnants. Perhaps most interesting of all, however, were the posters and instruction manuals that explained the shelter equipment and how it was to be used in case of attack.

The contents have been inventoried and preserved, and the shelter has been locked up securely once more. DOT does not expect that it will be opened or used again. At least not until it's time for the next bridge inspection.

A DAUGHTER'S LIBRARY

Where is a social justice library located?

Seattle has a well-deserved reputation as a socially liberal and progressive city, earned over decades. Seattle was the first major city in the United States to elect a female mayor, Bertha Knight Landes, back in 1926. It had the first living building, the Bullitt Center. And it pioneered a landmark minimum wage law ($15/hour) long before it was proposed nationally.

Inspired by his upbringing in a multicultural and multiracial setting, Edwin Lindo, an instructor on race and law at the University of Washington, wanted to inspire others. He wanted to pass on his values to his young daughter, Estella, and the community around her. Although Lindo had no bookstore or library experience, he decided to start a justice-focused community library and bookstore.

The library started inside the Wine Station, a small wine bar in the Beacon Hill neighborhood.

> ## ESTELITA'S LIBRARY
>
> **WHAT:** Library and bookstore
>
> **WHERE:** 2533 16th Ave. S.
>
> **COST:** Free to browse. Checking out books requires a membership ($30–$50/year).
>
> **PRO TIP:** Estella is now three years old.

It was no staid, stiff environment either. Estelita's was boisterous and full of life, much like its namesake. The library became a social hub for reading, listening to musicians and other artists, and creating a community for thought-provoking discussions. Soon speakers, debates, meetings, and classes were scheduled.

Lindo packed Estelita's limited shelf space with a curated collection of his books and made purchases from other libraries to round things out. The themes are evident—topics surrounding social justice, ethnic studies, and liberation movements. Browsing the shelves reveals a rich collection that delves deep

A peek inside the new location of Estelita's Library.

into the history of people of color: their struggles, philosophies, aspirations, and triumphs. The library is organized to encourage browsing and personal discovery rather than following a traditional library structure.

Estelita's recently moved to a new location in the Central District. There's room to build up the collection and community space. The large patio deck is perfect for relaxation and events, continuing to foster discussions and community activism.

Estella was only a year old when her father started a community library and bookstore, naming it after her.

WALKING THE LINE

Where is there an urban trail in South Seattle?

The Chief Sealth Trail is like an oasis in the desert for the urban residents of southeastern Seattle. Opened in 2007, the 3.5-mile greenbelt trail is named after Chief Sealth, for whom Seattle was named. He was a chief of the indigenous people who lived in the Puget Sound region.

Generally, the trail winds between gentle slopes and hills through the Beacon Hill neighborhood to Rainier Beach. It follows along the greenbelt beneath the power lines connecting Kubota Garden with Jefferson Park. It's tucked away; you'll need to look for it. Signage helps point the way, although the signs are small and tough to spot while driving. It's probably easiest to just look for the giant power lines and navigate from there. The trail is 10 feet wide, with a 2-foot gravel shoulder on each side, so there's room for cyclists and pedestrians.

The Chief Sealth Trail was constructed primarily from reused and recycled materials from light rail construction. Contractors used the soil and crushed concrete to build the pathway and create landscaping alongside it. It was an eco-friendly option, built more quickly and at a lower cost than entirely new construction.

You'll have the holy grail of Seattle views along the pathway—the Cascades, Lake Washington, Mount Rainier, and the Olympics. Plus, you can jealously ogle the vegetables in the P-Patches

Chief Sealth Trail is part of the regional trail system, one of five regional trails that promote healthy activities and connect schools, businesses, and residents.

Signage points you in the right direction on the Chief Sealth Trail.

(community gardens) along the way. Pay attention to the signage, though, as the trail can be confusing at some intersections. You're never far from signage or sight of the path.

There's room to grow, too. The Chief Sealth Trail will eventually link to downtown Seattle, the light rail station on Martin Luther King Way, and the Mountains to Sound Greenway.

CHIEF SEALTH TRAIL

WHAT: Regional urban trail

WHERE: Between South Ferdinand Street at Beacon Avenue South and South Gazelle Street at 51st Avenue South

COST: Free

PRO TIP: The trail is dog-friendly.

ALL THERE IS IS SKY

Where is there an aperture in the ceiling?

If you only think about aperture in the context of photography, Skyspace at the Henry will expand your view.

James Turrell, the renowned light and space artist, designed *Light Reign* to celebrate the 75th anniversary of the Henry Art Gallery at the University of Washington. The permanent installation is located in the sculpture garden and is a part of Turrell's Skyspace series. There are around 80 Skyspace installations around the world.

Like other Skyspace installations, *Light Reign* is an illuminated, enclosed circular space with an egg-shaped aperture in the ceiling. The exterior is distinctive, a lighting display that slowly changes and evolves. The lighting changes based on day and season and looks like an egg-shaped pleated lampshade.

Inside, there is an oval aperture in the ceiling. It's generally open but has a movable dome for the all-too-frequent inclement Seattle weather. When the dome is in place, it glows blue, simulating the sky. Look up. Gaze at the sky through the aperture. All you'll see is the sky—no buildings, no towers, no

SKYSPACE AT THE HENRY

WHAT: Art installation

WHERE: 4100 15th Ave. NE

COST: $10

PRO TIP: No two visits to Skyspace are the same. Weather and time of day change the experience.

Art. Architecture. Meditative space. All terms used to describe *Light Reign*, James Turrell's Skyspace at the University of Washington's Henry Art Gallery.

The exterior of Skyspace blends into the museum architecture until it comes alive with light.

construction cranes (that are seemingly reproducing themselves all over the Seattle skyline).

The effect is calming, almost meditative, even when other visitors are in the space. The experience is not merely what you are looking at in the sky, but also about your experience looking at the sky. Or, as Turrell says, "you are looking at you looking."

A GARDENING FAMILY

Where can you find a Japanese Garden?

Tucked away in south Seattle, Kubota Garden is a 20-acre park that combines Japanese garden design concepts with native Pacific Northwest plants. It is managed by the city's Parks and Recreation Department and the Kubota Garden Foundation.

The garden was started in 1927 by Japanese immigrant Fujitaro Kubota, who owned a gardening business in Seattle. Although developing a five-acre plot of swampland may seem like an ambitious project, the garden started as a hobby. A few years later, Kubota added more land, and the simple hobby turned into a significant commitment. In addition to serving as a home for the business, the garden became a cultural gathering spot for other Japanese immigrants.

Things changed after the bombing of Pearl Harbor with the issuance of Executive Order 9066, which required the removal of all persons of Japanese ancestry, whether citizens or resident aliens, from the West Coast. Kubota and his family were removed from Seattle and interned at the Minidoka War Relocation Center in Idaho. The garden and business had to be abandoned. During the four years that his family was interned, he oversaw the construction of a Japanese rock garden in a Minidoka community park.

When internees were finally released at the end of World War II, Kubota returned to Seattle, intent on resurrecting his gardening business, this time with help from his two sons. They successfully revived their business and reestablished the garden. Shortly before Kubota passed away, Japan awarded him the Fifth Class Order of the Sacred Treasure, honoring him for

---

Kubota Garden is a public park owned by the City of Seattle and is a historic landmark.

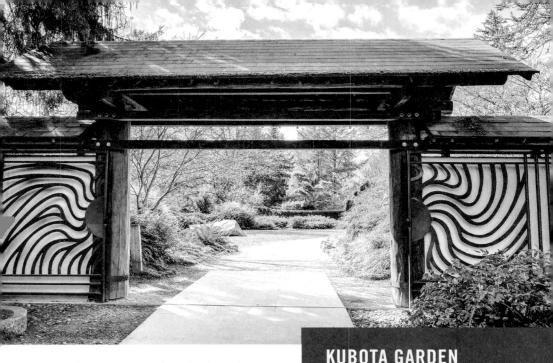

The entrance to Kubota Garden welcomes you to 20 acres of beautiful grounds.

KUBOTA GARDEN

WHAT: Park

WHERE: 9817 55th Ave. S.

COST: Membership is free and open to the public.

PRO TIP: You can see other gardens created by Fujitaro Kubota at Seattle University and Bloedel Reserve on Bainbridge Island.

his contributions in promoting Japanese gardening in the United States. He continued to maintain the garden until he died in 1973, and his legacy was passed on to another generation of family and community members.

A world war couldn't doom the garden, nor could years in an internment camp. But the garden was nearly done in by an urban development plan that threatened to build condominiums on the site. Community members rallied to save the park, and the City of Seattle purchased the property, including a section that had been declared a historic landmark.

The city maintains the garden in partnership with the nonprofit Kubota Garden Foundation. Through the public-private partnership, the spectacular landscape remains a tribute to its founder.

A SOUND GARDEN

Where are Seattle's grunge rock roots?

The word "grunge" may mean dirt or scum, but in the music world, it's synonymous with the "Seattle sound," the alternative rock sensation that gripped the world in the early 1990s. Many rockers take issue with the word, arguing it's not a genre at all but more of a mindset. Some bands even rejected the label, stating that the term obscured a variety of styles. Whether grunge emerged as a way to describe a deep, sludgy, rock riff–based sound or put a name to the darker themes it was addressing, it all began in Seattle with the band Soundgarden.

The Seattle sound is usually credited to Seattle independent record label Sub Pop. One of the label's co-founders, Jonathan Poneman, saw Soundgarden perform in 1987 and wanted to put out an album for the band. Sub Pop signed a contract with Soundgarden, releasing its first hit EP album, *Screaming Life*.

> ## SEATTLE GRUNGE
>
> **WHAT:** Music
>
> **WHERE:** Everywhere
>
> **COST:** Free
>
> **PRO TIP:** The late Soundgarden guitarist Chris Cornell once worked at Ray's Boathouse at Shilshole.

After Soundgarden, Sub Pop went on to work with other big bands from the Seattle grunge scene such as Nirvana, Tad, and Mudhoney, which later split to form Pearl Jam.

The label marketed a Seattle sound produced with cheap, quick, and consistent studio techniques. When this music hit the mainstream in the '90s, it changed the world's musical landscape and was dubbed "grunge rock." Soundgarden went on to sign with A&M Records, the first grunge band to sign with a major record label. Other major labels followed with signings of bands such as Alice in Chains, Screaming Trees, and Nirvana.

A statue of Soundgarden's Chris Cornell is located outside the Museum of Pop Culture.

Soundgarden became well-known with its 1994 album *Superunknown*, and two of its singles, including "Spoonman," won Grammy Awards. "Spoonman" honored a longtime Pike Place Market busker whose instruments of choice were spoons.

Grunge influenced everything from pop culture to runway fashion and set the tone for the post-grunge music that followed. Soundgarden is credited for its pioneering spirit and originality, and for putting the Seattle grunge scene on the musical map. Although other grunge bands like Pearl Jam and Nirvana attained more fame and popularity, none of it would have been possible without Soundgarden taking the first steps.

Soundgarden took its name from a public art installation, *A Sound Garden*, located on the National Oceanic and Atmospheric Administration grounds.

NEW ART IN TOWN

What's the newest art museum in Seattle?

The Museum of Museums (MoM) recently opened in a mid-century building on the Swedish Medical Center campus. The building is nondescript, looking exactly like what it once was—a medical office building and storage site. That's where the former look ends, however. Greg Lundgren, the museum founder, agreed to refurbish the building as part of taking it over and creating the new art museum. Swedish Hospital remains a sponsor of the museum.

The museum's mission is to increase participation in the arts and reinvigorate the local art scene—not just for art lovers but also for artists. Lundgren, a Seattle filmmaker and artistic entrepreneur, has created a space that is jam-packed with art, no matter which way you turn.

The museum has two exhibition areas and an additional three museums within the museum. It's easy to see how the museum got its name.

It's very early days at the Museum of Museums. A few themes are emerging, though, most notably challenging our notion of what a museum is and should be and how we want to interact with art. With an open-ended mission like that, visitors will want to visit often to see how exhibits and displays change.

The museum's long-delayed opening was in March 2021. Its first exhibits feature unexpected topics ranging from interactive installations dealing with witchcraft, magic, and art to one that feels like a virtual world providing an alternate reality tour.

The Museum of Museums (MoM) is a three-story contemporary art center located on Capitol Hill.

The cleverly named Museum of Museums is the newest addition to the list of Seattle art museums.

MUSEUM OF MUSEUMS

WHAT: Art museum

WHERE: 900 Boylston Ave.

COST: $10

PRO TIP: Pick up the double-meaning "I ♥ MoM" t-shirt at the gift shop.

The museum-within-a-museum concept features the Supperfield Contemporary Art Center, an exhibit of narrative miniatures. It's a little world all of its own centered around (fictional) museum founder Margaret Supperfield. The world is filled with miniature figurines and art provided by various Seattle artists. It's very meta in creating a narrative around the institutional drama of art museums.

A NEW KING IN TOWN

Who is King County named for?

King County is the most populated county in the state, and its county seat—Seattle—is the most populated city in the state. But there's much more to King County than Seattle. The county covers some 2,300 square miles and extends from Puget Sound (including Vashon Island) to the Cascades. The estimated population is around 2.2 million people, about a third of the total state population.

King County was originally named for William Rufus DeVane King, a senator from Alabama. King was elected the 13th vice president of the United States, but he died of tuberculosis six weeks later, before carrying out any duties of the office. He was also a slave owner.

In 1986, a motion was passed by the King County Council to name the county for Martin Luther King Jr. instead of William Rufus King. Instead of honoring a man who enslaved people, the council changed the county namesake to Martin Luther King Jr., who stood for justice and equality. Dr. King was a leader in the civil rights movement from 1955 until he was murdered in 1968. Influenced by the great political leader Mahatma Gandhi, he promoted nonviolence and civil disobedience while struggling for legal and social equality. He won the Nobel Peace Prize for achieving racial justice through nonviolent resistance.

KING COUNTY NAMESAKE

WHAT: History

WHERE: Official King County buildings and sites

COST: Free

PRO TIP: King County is nearly twice the geographical size of Rhode Island.

The King County logo, a stylized portrait of Dr. Martin Luther King Jr., appears on county buildings, signs, and official documents.

The change was not made official until 2005, though, as it required deliberation and action by the state legislature. Finally, Governor Christine Gregoire signed the bill passed by the state legislature, and the namesake change became effective on July 24, 2005. It was a statement of what King County wanted to be known for.

In 2007, King County changed its logo from a gold crown to a graphic image of Martin Luther King Jr. The same photo is used in the county flag, the photo superimposed on a green background.

Although the county's name remains the same, the change in its namesake reflects its commitment to equality and social justice.

OPPORTUNITY TO THRIVE

Where is the oldest Black-owned bookstore in Seattle?

More than 20 years ago, Vickie Williams had a lightbulb moment and started a bookstore dedicated to the Black community. Life Enrichment (LEMS) Bookstore opened as a safe space to discuss the African diaspora, then grew into a cultural hub for Seattle's Black community. It was a long journey, but LEMS has become a gathering space for book readings, author appearances, art shows, concerts, discussion groups, and educational workshops.

In 2017, LEMS was dealt a significant setback when founder Williams died, and the bookstore fell on hard times. The bookstore closed, leaving a hole in its Columbia City neighborhood and among its devoted followers.

Hassan Messiah, Williams's godson, committed to taking on the bookstore's management and worked round the clock to reopen it. An online fundraiser raised far more than the amount targeted to re-launch, and the additional money was targeted to increase the store's resources. A niece, who grew up in the store, came on board to handle day-to-day operations. Other bookstores helped out with donations of relevant used book titles to help build up the collection to over 1,000 used books. LEMS was back in business.

LEMS's reopening is still fresh. It doesn't even have a phone or website yet. The store has started collaborating with local schools and is building up its inventory of books, resources, and local

LEMS BOOKSTORE

WHAT: Bookstore

WHERE: 5023 Rainier Ave S.

COST: Free to visit

PRO TIP: Crowdfunding efforts raised over $93,000 to save the bookstore, nearly $20,000 over the goal. Donations are still appreciated.

LEMS bookstore only recently reopened and is gaining back its loyal supporters.

arts and crafts. Before reopening was possible, the store made appearances at local outdoor vending events, continually creeping toward welcoming customers.

Development and expansion plans for LEMS are ambitious. Rainier Avenue Clothing Company is moving in and will share the space. There are plans to build a stage for music, comedy, readings, and other community performances. There is room at the back of the area that's perfect for a recording and sound studio.

With all the changes, though, LEMS will always be true to its roots—a bookstore that provides resources to the Black community.

LEMS is the only Black-owned bookstore focused on the African diaspora in the Pacific Northwest.

KIDDING AROUND

How has the pandemic affected animals?

The quarantining and isolation of the pandemic have taken a toll on everyone. We've gone too long without contact with one another, and it's taken a toll on our bodies, minds, and souls. We may not want to talk about it, but it's been a tough loss.

Did you know that animals have been experiencing the same sense of loss as we have been? Not in the same way, of course, but they have an animal version of it. For zoo animals, a lack of visitors means a corresponding lack of stimulation. And while the zoo staff does everything it can to maintain the animals' mental health, the pandemic makes it difficult.

At Point Defiance Zoo & Aquarium, one of the tools to keep animals engaged is hands-on zookeeper experiences. These experiences have been offered for some time but have increased in importance when animals haven't seen regular visitors. These experiences aren't designed to make animals perform; instead, they are an attempt to integrate variety into what can be a very dull routine. It's a change in routine for zoo visitors as well.

Because it's suitable for most ages, the Groovy Goat experience has become a visitor favorite. It's a chance to meet the zoo's Nigerian dwarf goats, learn how the zookeepers take care of the goats, and help provide some additional stimuli for these charming herbivores.

The goats wear collars with their names on them—red collars for the girls, blue for the boys. They have names like Sugar, Bentley, and Sage, and they are eager to see you. They'll gently nudge and preen as you groom them, combing their hair and

---

Nigerian dwarf goats average around two feet in height and 75 pounds. They are a precocious breed.

Sugar is one of a dozen Nigerian dwarf goats living at Point Defiance Zoo & Aquarium in Tacoma.

GROOVY GOATS

WHAT: Zoo experience

WHERE: 5400 N. Pearl St., Tacoma

COST: $150 for a group of up to five, includes zoo admission. Zoo admission is $18 for adults, $14 for children.

PRO TIP: Tacoma Science and Math Institute, a public high school, is located within Point Defiance.

pampering them as if they were at a day spa. You'll soon discover who is the prima donna, who is the alpha goat, and who is sweet but shy.

The goat interaction includes a chance to feed them; it's a treat in addition to their regular feeding and nutrition schedule. Then you'll create some toys for the goats to play with, part of the enrichment program so vital to their continued well-being. And perhaps something crucial to our well-being also.

COLD WAR LAUNCH PADS

Where were the missiles located in Seattle during the Cold War?

When the Cold War raged, the Seattle area housed several missile defense installations. These advanced defense systems stood guard against the threat that Soviet missiles could reach the United States, with devastating results. Defense sites needed to be close to the cities and critical facilities that they protected, but they also required 119 acres of land for each location.

While exact details are still somewhat obscured, it's likely there were 18 Nike missile locations in the area surrounding Fairchild (Spokane), Hanford (Tri-Cities), and Seattle. In King County alone, there were probably seven Nike Ajax missile sites. The installations consisted of interceptor fighter aircraft and anti-aircraft firearms, aided by long-range radar systems.

Eventually the more advanced Nike Hercules missiles with nuclear warheads replaced the Nike Ajax. The new missiles needed less land (only 40 acres) for installation and were deemed more effective than their predecessors. This resulted in many of the previous Nike sites being closed.

COUGAR MOUNTAIN REGIONAL WILDLAND PARK

WHAT: Park

WHERE: 18201 SE Cougar Mountain Dr., Issaquah

COST: Free

PRO TIP: Due to safety hazards from historical mining activities in the park, you must stay on the trails identified on the map.

A Nike missile site was located in an open field near the Sky Country Trailhead in Cougar Mountain Regional Wildland Park.

A beautiful picnic and play area at Cougar Mountain Regional Wildland Park once housed Nike missile launch pads.

These decommissioned sites were sold off and eventually became parks, recreational grounds, military or government facilities, and private property. King County purchased sites in the Seattle Defense Area through a series of transactions from the 1960s to the 1980s.

One of the acquisitions was the Nike site on Cougar Mountain. Decommissioned in 1964, the area was annexed with surrounding property to create a 3,000+ acre regional wildland park. The park has four major trailheads and eight smaller ones that make 35 miles of trails. Maps are available and provide a necessary caution: "Due to safety hazards from historical mining activities in this park, you must stay on the trails identified on the map."

The trails wind their way through mature forests and past streams, wetlands, caves, and cliffs. Some parts of the park have views of Lake Sammamish, the Cascades, Seattle, and Bellevue, while other areas are more remote, isolated from the sights of urban development. There are five named waterfalls and numerous small, sometimes imperceptible ones.

The park is beautiful and pristine; most visitors never realize they are visiting an area whose original purpose was one of destruction. Cougar Mountain combines with adjacent Squak Mountain State Park to create the Issaquah Alps, over 5,000 acres of protected public land.

SWIMMING UPSTREAM

How do salmon leave Puget Sound to spawn?

Visit most Seattle restaurants, and you'll likely find salmon on the menu. It's one of the most popular seafood items in the city. Not only do salmon feature prominently on dinner plates, but they also play a critical role in the Pacific Northwest ecosystem.

Pacific Northwest salmon hatch in freshwater environments such as streams, rivers, and lakes, then relocate to salt water to grow to maturity. At the end of the life cycle, they migrate back to fresh water to spawn. During the summer months, salmon pass through the fish ladder at the Ballard Locks.

Built in the 1900s by the Army Corps of Engineers, the locks enable boats to move between the fresh waters of Lake Washington and the Puget Sound estuary, where fresh water and salt water mix. Officially named after Major Hiram Chittenden, the formal name is a mouthful, and most locals shorten the name and refer to the structure as the Ballard Locks after its location.

Recognizing that the fish needed to make this same transit, the lock design incorporated a fish ladder into its plan. The ladder enabled fish to pass between fresh and salt water just like boats do. Sockeye, Chinook, and coho salmon repeat life cycles by passing through the Ballard Locks to travel upstream to spawn.

The fish ladder consists of a 21-step gradual incline that forms the migratory path for salmon moving into fresh water. Once they go through the locks, the salmon travel close to

HIRAM M. CHITTENDEN LOCKS

WHAT: Locks and fish ladder

WHERE: 3015 NW 54th St.

COST: Free. There is also no fee for boats to pass through the locks.

PRO TIP: The best viewing time for salmon migration is July and August.

Coho salmon are one of several species that travel between salt and fresh water through the fish ladder at the Ballard Locks.

50 miles upstream, where they arrive at their breeding grounds in late September. The females lay thousands of eggs in the freshwater riverbeds, then die, releasing vital nutrients into the soil as their bodies decay. The eggs hatch three months later, and the process reverses as the next generation heads to salt water.

In 1976 the fish ladder was renovated to improve fish conservation and provide enhanced viewing opportunities for visitors. Underground salmon-viewing windows let visitors see fish swimming upstream through the ladder, while researchers get an up-close view of endangered fish and their behavior.

Although the salmon viewing rooms remain open all year long, summer is the peak period of salmon migration when you're likely to see thousands of salmon migrating.

The fish ladder at the Ballard Locks is part of the process that ensures a bountiful sea for our dinner plates and ecosystem.

THE LAST STONE COTTAGE

Where is the last stone house in West Seattle?

Historic buildings are an essential and often irreplaceable part of a people's history. They aren't without their problems, though—both practical and contextual. Like many cities, Seattle has lost several historic landmarks to commercial developments. But there's a happy ending for the last stone cottage in West Seattle.

The stone cottage dates back some 90 years. Eva Falk and her mother built the Depression-era stone house using carefully selected stones from the beach next to Alki Point Lighthouse. More than 15,000 stones were carted from the beach, a distance of two miles, then put in the hands of artisans. With a bit of cement, sand, and cream of tartar, the stones created a beautiful facade for the home.

EVA'S STONE COTTAGE

WHAT: Home

WHERE: 1123 Harbor Ave. SW (soon to be moved to temporary storage)

COST: Free—donations appreciated

PRO TIP: The Duwamish people believe that their ancestors' souls are in the stones in the cottage.

Eva was a gracious hostess by all accounts, frequently entertaining total strangers who stopped by to learn more about her stone cottage. She passed away in 1997 at the age of 92.

People don't want to live in stone cottages these days, though, no matter how spectacular the water and skyline view is. So it wasn't surprising that the lot the stone cottage sits on, along with two other adjacent ones, was purchased to develop a condominium complex. It made a lot more sense than leaving a vacant stone house on prime real estate. The cottage had a date with the wrecking ball.

The Southwest Seattle Historical Society launched a Save the Stone Cottage crowdfunding campaign. The multi-faceted campaign had the immediate goal of saving the cottage from demolition. Beyond that, the plan calls for moving the house to a secure location until

The cottage has been saved from demolition, but funds are still needed to preserve it.

a permanent parcel of property can be purchased. There will be additional expenses for securing property, paying for plans and permits, and moving it to a location where it can be preserved and opened to visitors. The developer has made a $20,000 contribution to the campaign and is involved in the preservation efforts.

An additional sense of urgency involved the Duwamish tribe, indigenous citizens of the land where much of Seattle was located (Chief Sealth was a member of the Duwamish nation). The Duwamish people believe that people's souls return to the earth and live on in trees, sand, and rocks upon death. The stones needed to be saved to save the souls of ancestors.

The stone cottage has been saved, but it's still early in the preservation process. Donations continue to be welcomed.

Eva's Stone Cottage will be moved to a storage location until funds can be raised to relocate and preserve it.

UFF DA!

Why did Scandinavian immigrants settle in Ballard?

Ballard was an independent city before it was annexed to Seattle in 1906. Like much of the rest of the region, the area that is now Ballard was home to the indigenous Duwamish people before settlers arrived and displaced them. Ballard, both the original city and the neighborhood after annexation, became known for its Scandinavian community.

Just as the Irish Potato Famine drove Irish immigration, so did famines in Scandinavia drive Norwegian and Swedish immigration. The fear and uncertainty of that time made it easier for immigrants to leave their homeland, yet they still searched for something familiar and comforting. In Ballard, they found it. It all centered around a maritime industry, especially fishing, that mirrored their homeland. By 1920, settlers of Scandinavian descent were the largest ethnic group in the state and exercised a powerful influence on their neighborhood culture.

As Seattle has expanded and sprawled over the years, the number of Scandinavian residents in Ballard has decreased. The nickname of Snoose Junction may have waned (snus was a tobacco powder product popular with Scandinavian settlers), but the neighborhood is still proud of its traditions and continues to celebrate and preserve Scandinavian culture.

Norwegian Constitution Day is observed on May 17, complete with big parades, music, and dances. Organizations like the Sons of Norway and Norwegian Ladies Chorus of Seattle preserve and promote Scandinavian heritage and culture. "Uff da," an

Ballard was formerly an independent city, with about 1,636 residents at the time of its incorporation in 1890.

The National Nordic Museum shares the stories of the five Nordic countries: Denmark, Norway, Sweden, Finland, and Iceland.

NATIONAL NORDIC MUSEUM

WHAT: Museum

WHERE: 2655 NW Market St.

COST: $18

PRO TIP: The University of Washington is widely regarded as having the best Swedish studies program in the United States.

exclamation of Norwegian origin used to express surprise, is Ballard's unofficial slogan.

The National Nordic Museum is located in Ballard and plays a significant role in celebrating and sharing Nordic culture. It may be largely overlooked by the non-Nordic community here at home, but it is well known worldwide.

The permanent exhibit depicts "Nordic Journeys." Four-thousand-year-old stone axes and Viking-era runes and tools give visitors a feeling of the scale of Nordic history, then fast forward to an exhibit of modern Nordic design and fashion. Through its artifacts and exhibits, the museum shares the stories of the Nordic people, both in their home countries and in the United States.

CASTLE ON A LAKE

Where can you stay in a castle?

Set on American Lake in Lakewood, Thornewood Castle was built about a century ago with bricks taken from a 15th-century English castle. Chester Thorne, a co-founder of the Port of Tacoma, shipped the bricks back to the Pacific Northwest to build the three-story, 27,000-square-foot castle. The stained glass window panels date back even further, to the 1300s.

The Gothic mansion was completed in 1911, and Thorne lived there with his family in opulent luxury. Extensive landscaping created a sunken English garden, the lake was suitable for fishing and swimming, and the surrounding 100 acres provided privacy. The Thornes entertained lavishly for wealthy guests, including two presidents.

When the senior Thornes died, the castle was left to their daughter, Anita, with instructions that it remain in the family. Anita disregarded her parents' request and sold the property. It was quickly sold and subdivided for home sites. Four acres and the lakefront were kept as part of the castle grounds.

THORNEWOOD CASTLE

WHAT: Bed and breakfast

WHERE: 8601 N. Thorne Ln. SW, Lakewood

COST: Room rates range from $300 to $500 per night.

PRO TIP: Thornewood Castle is a private residence in a gated community. It is not open to the general public, only guests with reservations. You'll need to stay if you want to see it.

Rumor has it that the Thornes were so upset the castle was sold that they refused to leave. There have been claims that ghosts of both Chester and his wife, Anna, have been seen. Chester's sightings seem to be related to light bulbs being unscrewed in what was his room. Sightings of Anna have occurred on the window seat in her former sitting room.

Thornewood Castle and estate from the formal garden. Photo by Joe Mabel, CC-BY-SA. joemabel.com

Castle ownership changed hands several times, and in 1982 the building was added to the National Register of Historic Places. By the time it was purchased by current owners Deanna and Wayne Robinson in 2000, the castle was starting to look a little shabby. Repairs and refurbishing were an expensive proposition. Funding was helped along a little by Hollywood—Stephen King's mini-series *Rose Red* was filmed at Thornewood Castle. Other movies filmed at the castle are *The Diary of Ellen Rimbauer* (a prequel to *Rose Red*) and *There Will Be Blood*.

Thornewood Castle is now an inn and event venue in addition to a private home. While maintaining its classic elegance, it has all the modern amenities expected in lodging. It remains one of the few authentic private castles in the United States.

Thornewood Castle was used for filming Stephen King's mini-series *Rose Red*. It has 28 bedrooms and 22 bathrooms.

X MARKS THE SPOT

Where can you find hidden treasure?

Finding new places to visit has never been easier than it is today. With just a few taps on the phone, endless lists of destinations, complete with ratings and reviews, become available. At the same time, having everything at our fingertips can dilute the spirit of exploration. Geocaching offers the best of both worlds—digital-age connectivity and the potential for unexpected discoveries.

In essence, geocaching is a real-time treasure hunt that can be done anywhere in the world. Dave Ulmer from Oregon created it in 2000 when he wanted to test the newly released GPS's accuracy, which the US government had made available to the public for the first time. He buried a bucket full of items in a field and posted the GPS coordinates. Within three days, two people tracked down the bucket. It was the beginning of geocaching.

The hidden treasures you seek out during a hunt are called geocaches. The traditional ones usually contain trinkets like a keychain, marble, or small toy, along with a logbook and some pencils. You can access websites to locate geocaches near you using an address, a geolocation code, or even a city name.

To start your treasure hunt, load the chosen cache's location into your GPS device, or use the app on your mobile phone, and off you go. When you discover a cache, you sign the

HIDDEN TREASURE

WHAT: Game

WHERE: Everywhere
Headquarters are at 837 N. 34th St., Ste. 300

COST: Free, although the mobile app has some upgrades available for purchase.

PRO TIP: Employees at Geocaching HQ created a guide to nine caches in their Fremont neighborhood. Pick up a passport at their offices.

Using the Geocaching app, you can look for hidden treasures close to home or when you are traveling.

logbook and either leave it as it is or exchange trinkets. It's a simple enough concept, but not always as easy as it sounds. Fortunately, some of the locations have tips and hints to help you out.

The adventure in geocaching is finding hidden treasure and seeing the world around you, learning a little something as you do. You can plan a geocaching scavenger hunt, randomly search when you're out and about, or connect with other cachers for group tours and treasure hunts.

Tours are offered at the Visitor Center, where you can also find the official Geocaching Headquarters geocache.

SOURCES

The People's Republic of Fremont: Site visit; fremontartscouncil.org; fremont.com

A Fishy Story: Site visit; dmhs.org; historylink.org

Be a Patches Pal: Site visit; jppatches.com; J. P. Patches: Northwest Icon by Bryan Johnston

Spreading the News: Site visit; louisahotelseattle.com; nwasianweekly.com/2017/09/a-trip-down-memory-lane; seattle.gov/Documents/Departments/Neighborhoods/HistoricPreservation/Landmarks/RelatedDocuments/chinese-community-bulletin-nomination-data-sheet.pdf

Now Hear This: Site visit; seattlepi.com/local/article/Phinney-neighbors-getting-air-raid-siren-restored-1217386.php; vintagewestwoodland.com/2016/04/02/seattles-second-bertha-cold-war-relic-on-phinney-ridge

A Haunted Brothel: Site visit; merchantscafeandsaloon.com; seattle.eater.com/2019/10/23/20928922/merchants-cafe-oldest-seattle-restaurant-bought-by-private-real-estate-firm

Stealing Is Wrong: Site visit; nps.gov/nr/travel/seattle/s26.htm; pcad.lib.washington.edu/building/4553

Party with an Elephant: Site visit and interview; seattletimes.com/seattle-news/auroras-aging-elephant-rises-again

Elevator of the Space Age: seattlemag.com/article/back-future-why-seattles-worlds-fair-mattered; seattlepi.com/lifestyle/article/Century-21-remnants-found-new-homes-1085219.php

The Play That Rocked Seattle: Site visit; nfl.com/news/fan-reaction-to-lynch-s-td-run-shook-area-by-qwest-field-09000d5d81d9815f; espn.com/nfl/story/_/id/10064056/epic-run-marshawn-lynch-reverberates-seattle; washington.edu/news/2015/01/07/how-the-beast-quake-is-helping-scientists-track-real-earthquakes

The Last Holdout: Site visit; eatballard.com/edith-macefield-house-up-house-in-ballard/; hollywoodreporter.com/news/seattle-up-house-movie-works-817335; anchortattoo.com

Singing Praises: Site visit; complinechoir.org; complineunderground.wordpress.com; www.knkx.org/post/after-63-years-women-sing-compline-seattle-cathedral

As Fast as a Greased Log Rolling Downhill: Sons of the Profit by Bill Speidel; Skid Road by Murray Morgan; nytimes.com/1986/12/02/us/a-clash-over-aid-effort-on-the-first-skid-row.html

A Woman with a Torch: Site visit; seattletimes.com/seattle-news/lady-liberty-will-make-strong-comeback-on-alki; seattlepi.com/local/article/Sea-Scout-leader-recalls-unveiling-of-Alki-s-Lady-1169719.php; westseattleblog.com/category/alki-statue-of-liberty

Icky Sticky: Site visit; unexpectedproductions.org/gumwall; edition.cnn.com/2009/TRAVEL/07/20/germy.tourist.spots; seattletimes.com/seattle-news/how-much-gum-dotted-pike-place-markets-post-alley

Ringy Dingy: Site visit and interview; telcomhistory.org/connections-museum-seattle; phworld.org/moc; king5.com/article/news/local/connections-museum-in-seattle-explains-how-we-communicate/281-574475727

Fins of Naval History: Site visit; faculty.washington.edu/jtyoung/fins.html; seattle.gov/parks/find/parks/magnuson-park

Teeming with Electricity: Site visit; seattle.gov/light/dennysub/substationdesign.asp; seattlemag.com/news-and-features/how-denny-substation-will-help-supply-seattles-growing-need-power-while-also

Let's Get (Meta) Physical: Site visit and interview; seattlemetaphysicallibrary.org; Margaret Bartley, President, Human Origins Book Club

Big Shoes to Fill: Site visit; guinnessworldrecords.com/records/hall-of-fame/robert-wadlow-tallest-man-ever; altonweb.com/history/wadlow

Vladimir Lenin Lives in Seattle: Site visit; fremocentrist.com/commentary/exhibiting-a-sense-of-humor-with-the-lenin-statue; seattletimes.com/seattle-news/lenin-statue-is-loved-hated-and-very-fremont

Candy Making History: Site visit; brown-haley.com; southsoundtalk.com/2017/03/17/the-sweet-smell-of-tacomas-chocolatey-past

Bruce Lee's Favorite Restaurant: taitungrestaurant.com; seattletimes.com/life/food-drink/seattle-restaurant-classics-why-you-need-to-go-to-tai-tung; king5.com/article/news/local/take-5/5-facts-about-bruce-lees-favorite-seattle-restaurant-tai-tung/281-c7787e0b-5a6c-4d40-99fe-82341e8eb8b5; https://brucelee.com

Cranes for Peace: Site visit; seattle.gov/parks/find/parks/peace-park; latimes.com/archives/la-xpm-2001-apr-29-me-57286-story.html

The Haunted Castle: Site visit; seattlemet.com/news-and-city-life/2008/12/1008-pastlives); seattletimes.com/pacific-nw-magazine/mom-and-son-revive-a-creepy-castle-in-georgetown; seanearley.com/the-georgetown-castle-a-paranormal-investigation; georgetownhistory.com/History/Homes/Gessner

Don't Forget to Visit Your Mummy: Site visit; yeoldecuriosityshop.com; seattlepi.com/news/article/Short-Trips-Store-piles-on-the-unusual-in-bits-1259124.php; archive.seattletimes.com/archive/?date=20010429&slug=mummy29m0

Get Your Exercise: Site visit; seattlestairwaywalks.com; theoutbound.com/washington/running/run-the-howe-street-stairs; rainorshineguides.com/blog/2017/5/7/seattles-outdoor-staircases

A Reach for Bike Safety: Washington State Driver Guide; wsdotblog.blogspot.com/2019/02/new-bicyclist-and-pedestrian-safety.html); dutchreach.org

What a View: Site visit; seattle.gov/parks/find/parks/kerry-park; seattlepi.com/ae/article/Doris-Chase-1923-2008-Artist-s-work-part-of-1295606.php

Can You Find the Time: Site visit; zombiezodiac.com/rob/ped/clock/citywide.htm; zombiezodiac.com/rob/ped/clock/map.htm

A Small and Spiteful House: Site visit; King County Assessor; komonews.com/news/local/seattles-iconic-pie-shaped-spite-house-is-back-on-the-market

It's Electrifying: Site visit and interview; seattle.gov/light/georgetownsteamplant; seattle.gov/light/georgetownsteamplant/history.asp

These Boots Aren't Made for Walking: Site visit; historylink.org/File/3480; seattle.gov/parks/find/parks/oxbow-park

A Literary City: seattlecityoflit.org; cityofliterature.nl/en/cities; spl.org

Pinups: Site visit; bettiepage.com; theatlantic.com/entertainment/archive/2014/01/male-fans-made-bettie-page-a-star-but-female-fans-made-her-an-icon/282794; mynorthwest.com/388227/bettie-page-house-mural-is-back

Eyes on You: Site visit; art.seattleartmuseum.org; theeastonfoundation.org; seattleartmuseum.org/Documents/Visit/2020-olympic-sculpture-park-map-and-guide.pdf

Pooh on Poo: Site visit; interview with Kaitlyn Welzen, Sustainable Waste Management Specialist, Woodland Park Zoo; zoo.org/zoodoo; seattletimes.com/seattle-news/with-a-new-modern-compost-facility-woodland-parks-zoo-doo-becomes-serious-stuff

Trailer Park Shopping: Site visit and interview; georgetowntrailerpark. com; thenewstribune.com/entertainment/article36077928.html; shotgunceremonies.com

A Metropolitan City: Site visit; www.hhof.com; seattle-metropolitans.com; nytimes.com/2017/03/27/sports/hockey/seattle-metropolitans-stanley-cup-seattle-ice-arena.html; seattlekrakenhockey.com

A Ghost Walked into a Bar: Site visit; kellsirish.com/seattle; irishcentral.com/culture/craic/ghost-america-haunted-irish-pub; ghostlyactivities.com/kells-pub-seattles-haunted-bar

Rubber Chicken: Site visit; archiemcpheeseattle.com; mcphee.com; seattletimes.com/pacific-nw-magazine/the-big-daddy-of-doodads-mark-pahlow-is-serious-about-archie-mcphee; seattlemet.com/style-and-shopping/20-essential-seattle-shops; seattlerefined.com/lifestyle/the-worlds-only-rubber-chicken-museum-is-in-seattle

Around the World: Site visit; seattle.gov/parks/find/parks/magnuson-park/history; historylink.org/File/2249; airandspace.si.edu/stories/editorial/first-flight-around-world-adventure-new-generation

Just Your Selfie: Site visit and interview; seattleselfiemuseum.com; seattlemet.com/arts-and-culture/2020/02/i-visited-the-seattle-selfie-museum-then-an-actual-museum; crosscut.com/2020/01/welcome-seattles-new-selfie-museum-where-you-are-masterpiece

Me Gotta Go: newyorker.com/culture/cultural-comment/jack-ely-louie-louie-the-dirtiest-song-of-the-sixties; louielouie.org

In a Pickle: usapickleball.org; pickleball.com/default.asp; globalpickleball. network/pickleball-courts/courts/city/255-seattle-washington

The Roar of the Falls: Site visit; interview with Alan Stephens; Washington Trails Association (wta.org/go-hiking/hikes/snoqualmie-falls); Seattle Southside (seattlesouthside.com/listing/snoqualmie-falls/286); City of Snoqualmie (ci. snoqualmie.wa.us/378/Snoqualmie-Falls); Salish Lodge & Spa (salishlodge.com)

Wedgwood Rocks: Site visit; wedgwoodinseattlehistory.com/2012/01/31/wedgwood-rock; northeastseattle.org/story-wedgwood-rock; king5.com/article/entertainment/television/programs/evening/wedgwood-rock-is-a-ravenna-neighborhood-icon/281-244541603; burkemuseum.org/news/mystery-wedgwood-rock

Overcoming a Toxic Past: Site visit; seattle.curbed.com/2019/4/12/18306264/gas-works-park-environmental-history; lakeunionhistory.org/Gasworks_History.html; apps.ecology.wa.gov/gsp/Sitepage.aspx?csid=2876

Hit the Trail: Site visit; traillink.com/trail/burke-gilman-trail; kingcounty.gov/services/parks-recreation/parks/trails/regional-trails/popular-trails/burke-gilman.aspx; wta.org/go-hiking/hikes/burke-gilman-trail

Silence in the City: Site visit; pioneersquare.org/experiences/waterfall-garden-park; ups.com

Let There Be Light: Site visit and interview; Mayflower Park Hotel (mayflowerpark.com/olivers-lounge); History Link (historylink.org/File/20320); Seattle Weekly (seattleweekly.com/home/olivers-lounge-marks-40-years-of-cocktails-and-culture); Washington Administrative Code (WAC 314-11)

Play a Mean Pinball: Site visit and interview; Seattle Pinball Museum (seattlepinballmuseum.com/home.html); Pinball News (pinballnews.com/sites/seattlepinballmuseum/index.html)

The Building That Lives: Site visit; Bullitt Foundation (bullitt.org); The Bullitt Center (bullittcenter.org); New York Times (nytimes.com/2011/10/05/realestate/commercial/seattles-bullitt-center-aims-to-be-energy-self-sufficient.html); The Guardian (theguardian.com/sustainable-business/seattle-bullitt-center-green-sustainable-building?newsfeed=true); PBS Newshour (archive.vn/20130704090209/http://www.netnebraska.org/node/853503)

Sinks Full of Hope: Site visit; University of Washington (arch.be.uw.edu/seattle-street-sink-prototype); Elizabeth Golden Architecture (elizabethgolden.space/projects/seattle-street-sink); The Stranger (thestranger.com/slog/2020/10/16/47549576/that-sink-in-the-ally-is-supposed-to-be-there); Clean Hands Collective (cleanhandscollective.org/seattle-street-sink)

The Roar of Thunder Boats: Interview with David D. Williams; site visit; Seafair (seafair.org); My Northwest (mynorthwest.com/12723/its-a-local-thing-hydroplanes-echo-through-seattle-history/); KUOW (kuow.org/stories/heres-why-old-seattle-obsessed-hydroplanes)

A Tribute to Fishermen: Site visit; interviews; Fishermen's Memorial (seattlefishermensmemorial.org); Port of Seattle (portseattle.org/places/seattle-fishermens-memorial)

Walking on Glass: Site visit, Sons of the Profit by Bill Speidel; Skid Road by Murray Morgan; KING5 (king5.com/article/entertainment/television/programs/evening/the-historic-glass-streets-of-pioneer-square-are-nothing-short-of-amazing/281-449090324); Seattle Magazine (seattlemag.com/city-life/backstory-how-pioneer-squares-purple-sidewalk-skylights-came-be); Alliance of Pioneer Square; KQUD (kqed.org/news/11791667/what-are-those-grids-of-

glass-in-the-sidewalk-and-why-are-they-purple); Saving Places (savingplaces.
org/stories/illuminating-the-path-forward-for-seattles-pioneer-square-prisms#.
YBh9d-hKiUk)

Franklin Delano Roosevelt's Train: Site visit, restaurant website
(seattleorientexpress.com); City of Seattle (web6.seattle.gov/DPD/
HistoricalSite/QueryResult.aspx?ID=2147012156;); The Stranger (thestranger.
com/seattle/the-crazy-things-that-happen-inside-orient-express/
Content?oid=20948673)

A Super Salesman: Site visit; Grit City Magazine (gritcitymag.com/2018/01/
singing-tacomas-praises-made-allen-c-mason-an-1890s-millionaire); The
Proctor District (theproctordistrict.com/historic-locations); Tacoma History
(tacomahistory.org/media/dynamic/files/189_AllenCMason_Dedication.pdf);
Tacoma Metro Parks (metroparkstacoma.org/place/puget-park)

It Floats: Site visit; Washington State Department of Transportation (wsdot.
wa.gov/Projects/SR520Bridge/About/BridgeFacts.htm); WSP (wsp.com/
en-US/projects/sr520-evergreen-point-floating-bridge); Structure Magazine
(structuremag.org/?p=10525); History Link (historylink.org/File/5419)

A Journey Completed: Site visit; Port of Seattle; Seattle Times (seattletimes.
com/seattle-news/finally-completing-the-journey-flight-261-memorial-unveiled-
at-sea-tac)

Music Slumber Party: Edgewater hotel (edgewaterhotel.com); Seattle PI
(seattlepi.com/local/article/Beatles-stay-at-Edgewater-helped-mark-its-
place-1305857.php); Louder Sound (loudersound.com/features/fishing-for-the-
truth-the-ever-changing-story-of-led-zeppelin-s-mudshark)

A Historic View: Site visit, interview, Smith Tower (smithtower.com); Seattle
Curbed (seattle.curbed.com/2017/10/11/16460198/smith-tower-manual-elevators-
automated); Geek Wire (geekwire.com/2017/end-long-ride-seattles-historic-smith-
tower-automate-elevators-century-manual-operation); Seattle Times (seattletimes.
com/business/real-estate/for-rent-the-penthouse-atop-smith-tower)

Keep Clam: Site visit; History Link (historylink.org/File/2499); Ivar's (ivars.com/
our-story); Eater (eater.com/2019/6/5/18642684/ivars-seafood-seattle-history)

Going Batty: Bats Northwest (batsnorthwest.org/index.html); Habitat for
Bats (habitatforbats.org); Washington Department of Fish and Wildlife (wdfw.
wa.gov/species-habitats/living/species-facts/bats); Northwest Natural Resource
Group (nnrg.org/mission-approach/); interviews

North to Alaska: Site visit, interviews, National Park Services (nps.gov/index.htm)

Bucket of Blood: Site visit; KIRO TV (kiro7.com/news/local/rumored-speakeasy-remnants-unearthed-in-notorious-wah-mee-building/717033189); Louisa Hotel (louisahotelseattle.com/history); Seattle Times (seattletimes.com/entertainment/visual-arts/prohibition-era-murals-discovered-during-renovations-of-former-louisa-hotel); History Link (historylink.org/File/20550)

Keep Jiving: Site visit; National Park Service; South Sound Magazine (southsoundmag.com/the-legendary-history-of-bobs-java-jive-lives-up-to-rumor-mill; New Tribune (thenewstribune.com/news/local/article25872394.html)

No Fallout: Site visit; interview with Scott S. Williams, WSDOT

A Daughter's Library: Site visit; Estelita's Library (estelitaslibrary.com); Seattle Times (seattletimes.com/life/theres-noise-theres-music-estelitas-is-not-your-average-seattle-library-its-a-space-for-community); Cross Cut (crosscut.com/2018/05/new-beacon-hill-library-activists-dream)

Walking the Line: Site visit; Seattle Department of Transportation; Seattle Outdoors (seattleoutdoorsinfo.com/hiking-and-biking/seattle-biking/seattle-bike-trails/chief-sea); Trail Link (traillink.com/trail/chief-sealth-trail)

All There Is Is Sky: Site visit; Seattle Refined (seattlerefined.com/lifestyle/take-your-meditation-practice-to-james-turrells-skyspace); Architectural Digest (architecturaldigest.com/story/james-turrell-art-around-the-world); The Henry Gallery at the University of Washington (henryart.org/exhibitions/light-reign-james-turrell-skyspace); James Turrell (jamesturrell.com/work/type/skyspace)

A Gardening Family: Site visit; Kubota Garden Foundation (kubotagarden.org/index.html); Seattle Parks & Recreation

A Sound Garden: Official Soundgarden website (soundgardenworld.com); Museum of Pop Culture (mopop.org); Rolling Stone (rollingstone.com/music/music-news/soundgarden-chris-cornell-seattle-statue-unveiling-734199); The Guardian (theguardian.com/music/musicblog/2008/oct/31/grunge); Variety (variety.com/2017/music/news/soundgarden-pioneers-seattle-nirvana-pearl-jam-1202434337); Sub Pop (subpop.com)

A New King in Town: King County government (kingcounty.gov); Metro King County government (metrokc.gov/exec/mlk/motion.htm); KIRO TV (kiro7.com/news/local/today-in-history-king-county-officially-renamed-in-honor-of-martin-luther-king-jr/941770559)

Opportunity to Thrive: KING TV (king5.com/article/news/effort-to-save-black-owned-bookstore-in-seattle-a-beloved-cultural-hub/281-2f1423f9-2f61-4c0c-b5c5-c0fcab7ad475; South Seattle Emerald (southseattleemerald.com/2020/12/21/historic-l-e-m-s-bookstore-reopens); Seattle Times (seattletimes.com/entertainment/books/seattles-longest-running-black-owned-bookstore-begins-a-new-chapter-in-columbia-city)

Kidding Around: Site visit, interview with staff; Point Defiance Zoo & Aquarium (pdza.org)

Cold War Launch Pads: Site visit; King County Parks and Recreation (kingcounty.gov/services/parks-recreation.aspx); Seattle PI (seattlepi.com/seattlenews/slideshow/Ghost-Towns-of-Washington-Redmond-s-Nike-Missile-83048.php); History Link (historylink.org/File/9711); King County Archives (bytesandboxes.org/2016/10/13/from-coal-to-the-cold-war-cougar-mountain-regional-wildlife-parks-former-nike-missile-sites)

Swimming Upstream: Ballard Locks (ballardlocks.org); Army Corps of Engineers (nws.usace.army.mil/Missions/Civil-Works/Locks-and-Dams/Chittenden-Locks/Fish-Ladder); Seattle Times (seattletimes.com/seattle-news/environment/seattle-as-museum-tourists-can-still-see-wild-salmon-at-the-ballard-locks-on-video)

The Last Stone Cottage: Site visit; Save the Stone Cottage (savethestonecottage.org); Seattle Times (seattletimes.com/seattle-news/saving-west-seattles-depression-era-stone-cottage-one-beach-stone-at-a-time); West Seattle Blog (westseattleblog.com/2021/03/the-stone-cottage-will-be-saved-volunteers-plan-first-mile-of-historic-houses-journey)

Uff Da!: Site visit; interviews; Seattle Municipal Archives; National Nordic Museum (nordicmuseum.org); My Ballard (myballard.com)

Castle on a Lake: Thornewood Castle (thornewoodcastle.com); Legends of America (legendsofamerica.com/wa-thornewoodcastle)

X Marks the Spot: Site visit, interview, Geocaching HQ (geocachinghq.com), Geocaching app

INDEX